NITA LELAND

THE CREATIVE ARTIST

A Fine Artist's Guide to Expanding Your Creativity and Achieving Your Artistic Potential

NORTH LIGHT BOOKS

Cincinnati, Ohio

The Creative Artist. Copyright © 1990 by Nita Leland. Printed and bound in Hong Kong.
All rights reserved. No part of this book may be reproduced in any form or by any electronic
or mechanical means including information storage and retrieval systems without
permission in writing from the publisher, except by a reviewer, who may quote brief
passages in a review. Published by Writer's Digest Books, an imprint of F&W Publications,
Inc., 1507 Dana Avenue, Cincinnati, Ohio 45207. First edition.

94 93 92 91 90   5 4 3 2 1

Library of Congress Cataloging in Publication Data

Leland, Nita.
    The creative artist : a fine artist's guide to expanding your creativity and achieving your
artistic potential / by Nita Leland.
        p.   cm.
    Includes bibliographical references.
    ISBN 0-89134-325-3
    1. Art—Psychology. 2. Creation (Literary, artistic, etc.)
I. Title.
N71.L37 1990   89-23072
701'.15—dc20   CIP

Cover illustration by Edward Betts. *Northcoast,* acrylic, 40″ × 50″. Photo courtesy of Midtown
Galleries, Inc., New York City. Private Collection. *Road Trip* (21″ × 15″) by Robert Barnum
on title page. *Ocean Currents* (18″ × 26″) by Esther Grimm on dedication page. *Pine Island
Key* (12″ × 18″) by Sharon L. Stolzenberger on table of contents page.

DEDICATION

If you are:
—a beginner who wants to be a creative artist
—an artist who wants to be more creative
—a creative artist who is stuck
This book is dedicated to you.

ACKNOWLEDGMENTS

Because of some wonderful people, writing this book on creativity for artists has been a fantastic experience. First of all, my thanks to the sixty-six artists whose work appears on these pages, with special appreciation for the exceptional generosity of Joseph Barrish, Paul Melia, Sharon Stolzenberger, Elaine Szelestey, Virginia Lee Williams, and Brian Zampier. My thanks also to my editors, Greg Albert, Linda Sanders, and Lynn LaRue—in fact, to everyone at North Light Books—for their enthusiastic support. A word of appreciation to Diane Coyle and John Hill for their helpful critiques; to DeEarnest McLemore; to my students at Riverbend Art Center; and to my parents, family, and friends for their patience.
And, especially, to R.G.L.

CONTENTS

BIG PINE KEY 5/33

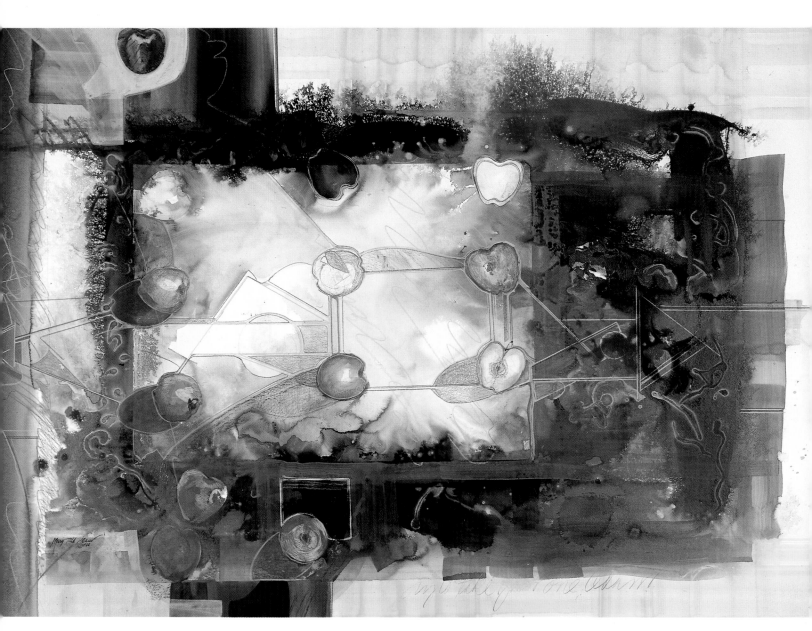

Starting out with random lines and flowing paint, Mary Beam then superimposes image and design on this creative painting. The artist's intuitive actions are controlled by her knowledge of how to make the picture work.

Sacred Circuit by Mary Todd Beam. Mixed media on Crescent board, 40" x 60". Collection of Michael and Donna High.

Introduction: Choose to Be Creative

"Creativity is a celebration of one's grandeur, one's sense of making anything possible. Creativity is a celebration of life — my celebration of life. It is a bold statement: I am here! I love life! I love me! I can be anything! I can do anything!"

Joseph Zinker, therapist, painter, sculptor, and poet

Choose to be creative! Creative people are curious, flexible, persistent, and independent, with a tremendous spirit of adventure and a love of play. Develop and strengthen these traits in yourself and reach your potential as an artist. This book will show you how.

Almost anyone can become a creative artist. The late Edgar A. Whitney, America's oft-quoted teacher of watercolor, said, "No door is closed to a stubborn scholar." What it takes is desire, determination, and perseverance.

Academic training is useful, but not essential. Many creative artists are self-taught, energized by the desire to create and a willingness to take chances. Creative people relish the discovery of ideas, new directions and challenges, and

the belief that there is another wonderful adventure just around the corner. Every human being has creative powers. You were born to create. Unleash your creative energy and let it flow.

What you believe you can be is what you will become!

Every artist in the history of art started out as a beginner. Your level of skill right now doesn't matter. You'll learn. Learning and doing cultivate creativity.

It doesn't necessarily take talent. Henri Matisse said:

It would be a mistake to ascribe this creative power to an inborn talent. In art, the genuine creator is not just a gifted being, but a man who has succeeded in arranging for their appointed end, a complex of activities, of

Hacker has captured Whitney "to the life," demonstrating a design principle to a workshop group. Some famous "Whitney-isms" appear in the background. *Edgar A. Whitney* by Homer O. Hacker, A.W.S. Watercolor, 21 ½" x 28 ½". Collection of the Ohio Watercolor Society.

which the work is the outcome. *The artist begins with a vision—a creative operation requiring an effort. Creativity takes courage.*

Creativity is more than "making a picture." Your art begins with a concept: your idea, your interpretation of the essential qualities of a subject. You work with the formal elements of design and use your craftsmanship and creative energy to shape your concept into a unique form. ***Creative art is what you make from your mental images and inner feelings.***

All this doesn't happen in a flash. Psychologist A. H. Maslow writes in *The Farther Reaches of Human Nature*:

Apparently one impression that we are making . . . is that creativeness consists of lightning

striking you on the head in one great glorious moment. The fact that the people who create are good workers tends to be lost.

That's good news! Creativity isn't magic. It's achievable! So don't wait for a "bolt from the blue." Find out what works for you, then get going. Start by asking yourself:

- What motivates me to undertake a creative challenge?
- What is my most creative environment?
- What is my most productive time of day?

This book will help you to inch around—and sometimes to leap over—roadblocks and strengthen your creativity as you exercise your skills. This isn't work—it's play! Have a good time doing it!

Making art should be fun. You can sense that the artist enjoyed developing this amusing image. Your attitude toward your art will always find its way into your work. *Mad as a Wet Hen* by Jan Upp. Watercolor, 21″ x 13 ½″.

This artist was inspired to craft a series of paintings using pure, bright colors and decorative patterns based on a simple theme: chairs. You don't need an exotic subject for a picture to be successful. *Untitled,* from "Chair Series" by Mel Meyer, S.M. Acrylic on canvas, 60″ x 60″.

Off to a Good Start

You don't need exotic materials to begin with. The humble pencil is the artist's best friend — a simple, familiar tool. So start with a ream of typing paper and a pencil.

Use your paper freely. Don't be intimidated by white paper or canvas. Take a fresh sheet of paper. Step on it. Fold it or crumple it. Let the cat walk on it. Brush it off and draw something on it. Isn't that easy? Treat every new support as you would any old piece of paper.

You will also benefit from trying different mediums, colors, and tools. You can do that with a minimum of expense by having a "flea market" with other artists to swap art supplies. Nearly every artist has an accumulation of materials collecting dust in the studio. One or two new "toys" may be just the thing to stimulate a creative change.

Another way to experiment is to invite a group of artist friends for a "painters' potluck." Ask each artist to bring a different medium, paper, or tool to share. Specify "something that will work with oils," "compatible with water-based mediums," or "anything that will make a mark on paper." Switch mediums and tools several times during the session. Pass a picture around during a painting session and let everyone have a hand in it.

You'll need a variety of objects for drawing and painting activities. Make a *treasure chest* out of a shoe box. Collect small objects for sketching: shells, nuts, leaves, buttons, driftwood, stones, weeds, nails, keys. Ask your family and friends to contribute "sur-

prises" to your collection.

In another box, your *collage box*, place odds and ends of art papers, wrapping papers, magazine pictures, bits of newspaper, ribbon, fabrics, lace, string, yarn, old paintings and drawings. You'll use these in some of your activities.

As you read through this book, you'll get many ideas for projects. To keep them from getting away from you, make a *job jar* from a cookie jar or a large bowl. On slips of paper, note activities from this book you would like to try. Drop in other ideas, subjects, or techniques to try. When you need a jump start, pull out a "job" at random and work with what's on the paper.

The first time I saw an Alex Powers watercolor, I was amazed to find marks, spatters, and gouges all over the paper. Instead of spoiling the picture, they added energy by revealing the artist's intensity and involvement with the subject. You will find similar treatment in this painting. *Fish Sale I* by Alex Powers. Watercolor, charcoal, and white crayon, 30" x 22". Collection of Jane and Harry Charles, Myrtle Beach, South Carolina.

Sketchbooks

If you don't already have one, go out right now and get yourself a sketchbook—your travelog on your journey into creativity. Spiral-bound, hardcover, loose-leaf, big or small, there are a lot of acceptable books in stores that sell stationery and school supplies. Keep a couple of sharpened #2 pencils and a pen with your sketchbook/journal—a ballpoint or inexpensive cartridge pen is fine. Spend fifteen minutes a day with your journal.

- Write notes to yourself.
- Make lists of ideas and creative projects.
- Copy inspirational quotes.
- Work out some of the activities suggested in this book.
- Doodle and draw.
- Sketch on location.
- Plan pictures.

Get it down before it slips away!

Graphic designer Brian Zampier, an avid sketcher, follows three simple rules:

- Never erase.
- Never tear out a page.
- Date every page.

These are great ideas! Use your sketchbook faithfully every day and follow Zampier's rules. A well-used sketchbook/journal is a creative artist's best friend.

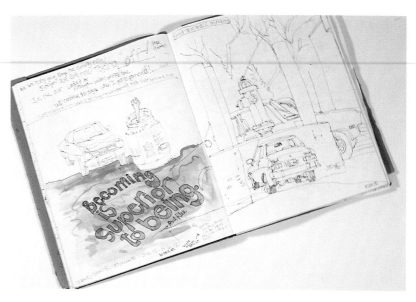

Preparing for the Journey

Provide yourself with a special art space where you are relatively free from interruption. Nothing elaborate is needed. As a young mother of four, I began painting and drawing at the kitchen table. This proved to be impossible with busy, hungry helpers all around me, so I moved to a card table in my bedroom. It was a little cramped, but at least I didn't have to wash peanut butter off my brushes! Now I have a wonderful, well-equipped studio, but I still think some of my most creative thinking was done in that special little art space!

Establish an atmosphere that stimulates you. Some artists flourish in confusion; others need to be free from interrup-

Artists use their sketchbooks in a variety of ways. Brian Zampier fills his with pen and ink gesture and contour drawings, notes, and comments (shown above). Jan Upp does colored pencil drawings of every imaginable type of daisy from every possible angle—a "theme" sketchbook. I make pencil value sketches for planning and reference, and Joseph Barrish makes marker drawings of trips and planning sketches.

This cubist-style print contains the image of a calico cat. Emily Karaffa bypassed realistic interpretation and represented the multi-colored patterns of the cat's fur in a black-and-white abstract design. *Cat Slumber* by Emily Karaffa. Intaglio print, 9 ¾" x 7".

tion. Many prepare themselves for work by exercising to stimulate circulation; others use meditation to quiet the chatter of the outer world. Find the method that suits you.

Make time for your art. Schedule it on your calendar and work other activities around it. Start with fifteen minutes a day. Even this short time will help you to improve your skills. As you gain confidence, you will feel less guilty about "wasting time" with your art. Believe me, you're not!

Allow some warm-up time each day to stimulate the creative flow. Scribble, doodle, draw, or splash a little paint before you start the day's project. It takes a few minutes to move from the "real world" into a creative mode. When you finish for the day, write a note reminding yourself of what you plan to do next. This helps you to remember today's super-

terrific idea when you get back to work tomorrow!

Hold off on judgment for a while. Use self-critique as a means of understanding rather than an opportunity for finding fault. You are hardest on yourself just when you need the most reassurance. As your skills and confidence improve, you'll be able to handle criticism and self-critique.

The emphasis in this book is on developing creativity through sensitivity, awareness, and determination. In each chapter I suggest activities to help you develop these traits. You make the creativity happen by doing the activities. Pick the ones you like and do them right away.

Take a creative trip starting today. Explore new territory. Enjoy the familiar highways and byways as you go along, but investigate new paths as well. Instead of crashing into

roadblocks, look for interesting detours around them. Curiosity and a willingness to experiment make an exciting journey.

Enjoy the trip, not just the destination. Before you arrive, you will already be thinking about your next trip!

Are you worried about inspiration? Don't be. It will come as you work.

Getting started is the hard part! James Russell Lowell said, "In creating, the only hard thing is to begin."

Don't just think about it. Don't just talk about it. **Do it!**

An art studio would be great, but you can make art almost anywhere. A desk or table will do. It helps to have good lighting. Look around the house for a likely spot for your "studio" and familiarize yourself with it by making a drawing of it.
Desk and Lamp by A. Brian Zampier, S.M. Pen and ink, 13 ½" x 21".

Simply stated, this is a snow scene with trees. If these words were all it took to describe a scene, we wouldn't need the picture. But words aren't adequate to express the beauty that Bob Frank sees in nature. The creative artist expresses things visually so we can see them, too. *January Shadows* by Robert Frank. Pastel, 19" x 25".

Chapter 1
Creativity: A Joyride

"People who want to be creative, who deeply value such a characteristic in themselves, are more likely to make themselves creative and keep themselves that way. . . . Creativity concerns what we do with our abilities. Any normal person can be creative in terms of whatever abilities he or she has or can acquire."

D. N. Perkins, The Mind's Best Work

Thinking you have no talent can be a self-fulfilling prophecy. "Argue for your limitations and sure enough, they're yours," says author Richard Bach in *Illusions*. So true! A positive attitude accelerates your development as a creative artist. When you believe in yourself, you can release and regulate the flow of your inborn creative energy to reach your artistic potential.

Emphasize the joy of creating, rather than the achievement of results. Artist/teacher Robert Henri said, "What we need is more sense of the wonder of life and less of the business of making a picture."

Develop your skills. Skills build confidence, so work to improve your drawing and refine your painting techniques. As Edgar Whitney said, "The discipline endured is the mastery achieved." You will improve with practice. While you're working, notice the good things you've done — don't dwell on mistakes. Set achievable goals: a confident

line, effective use of values, interesting shapes. Stay with it. You're sure to succeed.

Expand your horizons. Look at artwork in galleries, museums, and art fairs. Read books and magazines. Use your senses. Experience stimulates your memory and imagination.

Make creative thinking a part of your daily life. Ask questions. Vary routines. Do the unexpected. Change starts your creative juices flowing and makes you more observant of what's going on around you. You feel more mentally alert. Have you surrendered your creativity to television? Then turn the TV off! Pick up your sketchbook instead. Creativity becomes more accessible when you learn to act more impulsively in your everyday life.

Smash creative blocks. Change the problem or sneak up on it from a different direction. Try something fresh — a new way with an old theme, a different point of view, an unusual instrument.

Isn't this an unusual and visually exciting way to approach a floral subject? The careful patterning of the surface of the picture is unique to this artist. Such a painstaking method may not be your way, but your way will be revealed as you work with new ideas. *Street Bouquet* by Juanita Williams. Acrylic, 30" x 14". Collection of the artist.

Hippokantlerrelogriff

This child's marker drawing shows the intuitive creativity that is the first level of expression.

Skillful use of traditional mediums and techniques indicates the second level of creativity. *Street Scene with Balloons* by Serge Hollerbach. Acrylic on canvas, 40″ x 40″.

You Can Get There from Here

You probably take for granted the many creative things you do every day. Planning a banquet, organizing a business event, designing a database, decorating a room, even choosing the clothes you wear are all endeavors that reward you with feelings of accomplishment. When you feel really good about something you have done, it is because you have done it creatively. *You have always been creative.*

Changing daily routines is one way to access creativity. When was the last time you used a new ingredient in an old recipe? Walked through a garden? Sketched at a nature center? Designed a quilt?

Creative adventure is both exhilarating and demanding. *Art doesn't just happen—you make it happen.* You can get started by taking a class, reading a book, visiting another artist's studio. Pace your creative growth by taking a few short steps, then a big creative leap.

Creativity also requires flexibility and a willingness to change. It takes courage and the positive belief that you can do it.

Make up your mind to go for it! Make a conscious decision to give your art priority over other things. You can do it!

You can master drawing and design. You can do collage, or learn watercolor or oils. You owe it to yourself to put your creative development at the top of your list.

Creativity Can Be Learned

At one time the consensus was that creativity was an inborn characteristic of a few lucky people. If you weren't born with it, forget it. Now theories of creativity recognize the creative potential of every human being. What's more, they recognize that you can increase your level of creativity with a little effort.

I. A. Taylor defined five levels of creativity in "The Nature of Creative Process." (P. Smith, ed. *Creativity.* New York: Hastings House, 1959.) The first four levels of creativity can be attained by anyone with motivation.

1. The first level incorporates the *primitive and intuitive* expression found in children and in adults who have not been trained in art. There is an innocent quality to primitive art, but also directness and sensitivity. The naive artist creates for the joy of it.
2. The second level of creativity is the *academic and technical* level. At this level the artist learns skills and techniques, developing a proficiency that allows creative expression in myriad ways. The academic artist adds power to expression through mastery of craft.

The inventive artist finds unusual ways to manipulate ordinary materials, as Emslie has done here. *The Clansmen* by Sally Emslie. Acrylic on paper, 24" x 48". Collection of Mr. and Mrs. Warren Klink, Hamilton, Ohio.

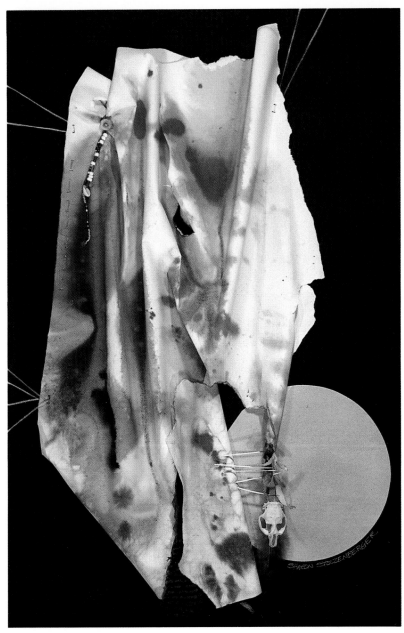

An innovative artist, Stolzenberger uses bones, beads, and feathers creatively to make distinctive art. *Artifacts from Feast of the Hunter's Moon* by Sharon L. Stolzenberger. Paper, watercolor, muskrat skull, porcupine quills, bone buttons, turkey feathers, wax-covered cord, and beads, 30" x 22".

3. Many artists experiment with their craft, exploring different ways of using familiar tools and mediums. This heralds the level of *invention*. Breaking rules is the order of the day, challenging the boundaries of academic tradition, becoming increasingly adventurous and experimental. Inventors use academic tradition and skills as a stepping-stone into new frontiers.

4. At the level of *innovation* the artist becomes more original. Materials and methods that are out of the ordinary are introduced. Now the artist breaks the boundaries. The academic foundation remains as a substructure of unconscious thought guiding these creative efforts.

5. The fifth level of creativity is characterized as *genius*. There are individuals whose ideas and accomplishments in art and science defy explanation. Genius is arguably the one level that is unexplainable and perhaps unattainable, something that an individual is born with.

Become a Child Again

Children quickly notice anything that is new and unusual; they explore it and then rush off to another adventure. A creative adult asks questions and takes chances, too. Researchers note that the child-like and playful attitude of many creative people is accompanied by an amazing flow of enthusiasm and energy. You can recover some of the creative energy you enjoyed as a child!

Children have few doubts about themselves as inventors, storytellers, and image makers. To a small child, anything seems possible. Do you remember the creative things you did when you were small? You made a clubhouse out of a box, cut paper dolls from cardboard, invented games and stories. The world was your playground. And it still is!

To tap into that natural creativity, try to recapture your childlike enthusiasm for everything around you. Work with the reckless abandon of a child. You may be able to call up the child within you by using materials you've long since abandoned—crayons, finger paints, chalk, construction paper—or by drawing while lying on the floor. Go ahead! It'll feel good to act like a kid again.

The Creative Adult

As an adult, you have many personal resources to draw upon in addition to a child's playful attitude. Your hopes and dreams, as well as your perceptions of the world around you come through in your work and make it unique.

Creative expression is not just a means of getting attention, although some have approached art that way. Think of art as a way of connecting, of sharing your insights with others.

Your viewers bring past experiences and prejudices to the work, perceiving more than a simple image. Your

Activity

On a sheet of illustration board or heavy white cardboard, start an autobiographical collage. Include memories of yourself as a child, your perception of yourself in the present, and your hopes for the future. Include things you like and things you hate. Glue on magazine pictures, draw, paint, or use real objects if they're not too big. Use crayons, colored pencils, watercolors, ink, whatever you like. There is no right or wrong way to place the pieces. As you fill up one sheet, start another. Use the collages as reference files for creative imagery.

Here is a partially completed autobiographical collage, including places I've been, things I love, and a few activities I enjoy. I decided to start another that shows what my art means to me. Several of the pictures on this collage have already inspired paintings.

viewers react intellectually to how you have made the work — your techniques and materials. Their senses respond to the way it looks and feels. But at a deeper level, they respond to the expressive content of the piece: to what you are saying. You express visually something that is inexpressible in words, something that relates to human experience. The source of this communication is yourself, so in order to be creative you must get in touch with yourself. The fountain of creativity begins with the stream of unconscious thought flowing inside you. Open the floodgate and creative ideas come rushing out.

Discover Your Themes

In *Fire in the Crucible* John Briggs highlights the importance to creative people of a *commitment to themes* that begins in childhood and continues throughout adult life. Each of us possesses a singular interest in specific ideas, although we may not be aware of their importance to us. Some typical themes are the relationships of human beings to each other, to animals, or to the environment; the phenomena of nature and science, metaphysics, or religion.

A theme may suddenly surface and pique your curiosity, raising fascinating questions that stimulate your creativity. If you aren't open to it, the theme may become lost in the shuffle of daily activity. What-

Birds often appear in my work unbidden. I started this painting by flowing watercolor washes diagonally across the page, but they turned muddy on me. I tossed the paper into the bathtub and took a scrub brush to it, mostly out of frustration. The marks and stains that remained after most of the pigment washed off reminded me of a bird, so I used that as the focal point for *Encounter*. *Encounter* by Nita Leland. Watercolor and ink, 22" x 30".

ever direction your life may take, the underlying themes remain. Discovering and exploring your themes open the way for rich creative development.

One of my themes developed from an early fascination with birds in the fields and woods in my neighborhood. This theme has endless variations: freedom (flight), spaciousness (the sky), delicacy (tiny songbirds), power (birds of prey), motion (flight), direction (upward), survival (hunting), beauty (color, feathers, wings). Any such theme can be expanded and interpreted in realistic or abstract art, developed in series or individually.

Activity

Search your autobiographical collage for your themes. Are there repeated images of people? animals? buildings? water? flowers? Do you find connections between themes — animals and natural surroundings, people and cities? When you recognize a theme, explore it. Are the people isolated in the city or part of the hustle and bustle? Are the animals in a domestic home setting, prowling a wild habitat, or endangered by an environmental hazard? Look beneath the surface of an image to find out why this theme is important to you.

Choose one theme from your autobiographical collage and develop it in a collage, painting, or drawing.

The network of spots on a slab of leopard agate was the starting point for this picture. Denington-Anderson enjoys designing abstracts based on colorful rock forms. What she sees in the rock is filtered through both conscious and unconscious processes during the incubation stage of creation to become the image captured on paper. *Agate VII: The Flame in the Stone* by Gayle Denington-Anderson. Watercolor, 22" x 30".

The Creative Process

There are definite steps in the creative process. Sometimes you work systematically through a creative project over a long period of time and other times you get instantaneous results; but either way the creative process is virtually the same.

The creative process begins with *identification* of the problem to be solved: selecting a subject to draw or paint, or mastering a new medium. Nothing creative can happen until you recognize what you want to do.

A *preparation* phase follows, during which you evaluate many possible solutions. At this stage you consider what you have done previously with similar problems or what other artists have done. You make thumbnail sketches, plan color schemes, and establish bound-aries for your creative activity. This is the thinking stage of the project.

In the *incubation* stage, you put the project on the shelf for a while. The information you accumulated in the preparation stage is sorted and assimilated in your unconscious mind. This stage may take only minutes while you set up to paint or take a coffee break. Then again, it may take a much longer time for a fully realized solution to surface.

Breakthrough is the fourth stage in the creative process, when the solution becomes immediately apparent. What comes to you is not "inspiration," but the result of your earlier thinking.

Once the breakthrough has occurred, a *resolution* step completes the process. You're ready to try your solution and see how it works.

Imagine That!

When you look out at the snow and wish you were walking on the beach, you are imagining. Everybody has imagination!

Imagination is the picture in your mind of something that isn't there. The creative artist takes those pictures out of the mind and puts them on paper or canvas, sometimes literally, sometimes symbolically. Poet Wallace Stevens describes imagination as "the power of the mind over the possibilities of things." You have the power to free your imagination.

Do you see figures in the shapes of moving clouds? When I was a little girl I saw a pair of Spanish dancers in an old oak tree, and when the wind blew, they danced for me. Look for people and animals in old stone walls, find images among shells washed up on the beach, see what the patterns on fences and weather-beaten boards suggest to you. Ordinary objects have extraordinary patterns and textures that can get your imagination rolling.

Some people have difficulty seeing pictures in their mind's eye. Don't expect to see complete images. If you have trouble starting with pictures, play word games and make marks that stimulate imagery. Many words suggest symbolic images that are easily represented by "marks" rather than pictures.

Take fifteen minutes every day to work on freeing your imagination. You won't be wasting your time. *Relaxed attention* is one of the most important states of mind for creativity and sometimes it has to be learned.

Find a quiet place where you will be free from interruptions for a few minutes. Practice vis-ualizing things in new and unusual juxtapositions. The unexpected gives you little shocks that sharpen awareness and enhance creative thinking. Visualize common objects in odd combinations or unusual places. A lemon with an umbrella. A typewriter on the beach. A palm tree and a penguin. This isn't a picture-making exercise. It's a way of stretching your creative muscles, like a jogger stretches before running. Occasionally, a visual idea that presents itself will have picture possibilities. When that happens, sketch it out and play with it for a while.

Let yourself daydream sometimes. Empty your mind of the

The objects in this painting are pictographic symbols rather than realistic representations. Smith calls them "autobiographical writings" and organizes them into a thematic composition that is highly suggestive of memories of childhood. *Boot* by Jaune Quick-to-See Smith. Acrylic and pastel on paper, 30" x 22". Courtesy of DEL Fine Art Galleries, Taos, New Mexico. Photography by F. A. Ambrose, Albuquerque.

thoughts that rush through it every waking moment. When this distracting "clutter" surfaces, let it go. Allow spontaneous images to come and go. Capture one in a quick sketch. Think about this image. Is it related to one of your themes? These images express your connections with your inner self. That's what creativity is about.

It's hardly likely that Jim Brower came upon this assortment of old neckties already beautifully arranged in an interesting composition. Instead he used his imagination to turn his heap of cast-offs into a mental picture and then developed this mental image into a skillful painting. *More Candidates for Goodwill* by Jim Brower. Transparent watercolor, 22" x 30".

Activities

• Close this book and make marks in your sketchbook/journal that express one or more of these words: angry, joyful, peaceful, sad, grieving, bored, excited, silly, serious. Are your marks similar to mine?

• Make a list of words that have strong visual or emotional connotations for you:

a descriptive word—elegant, harsh, wiry, frantic, dreamy, weird, turbulent

an action word—tumble, jump, skip, roll, flow, attack

the name of something you like—kittens, flowers, pizza, mountains

the name of something you fear—snakes, heights, spiders

a feeling or mood—excitement, conflict, passion, rage

Write one of the words in your journal or on a sheet of typing paper. Now "write" the word in a new way: Close your eyes and move your pencil around the paper, making marks that "feel like" the word. Swing your arm, stab at the paper, or caress the page to describe the word.

Choose another word from one of the categories above and write a word picture of it. When you consider

a subject to draw, think of words like these and the lines or movements you can use to "write" them in your pictures.

Word pictures are what you create by "writing" a word in a new way.

Pictorial word symbols like these are a universal language.

Brainstorming

Brainstorming generates ideas and visual images. When you're stuck, list words that come to mind spontaneously, no matter how unrelated they may seem to the matter at hand—the crazier, the better. Psychologist A. H. Maslow says, "If you are afraid of making (a) crazy mistake, then you'll never get any of the bright ideas, either." The most impractical idea may turn out to be the most useful one. In the early stages, reject nothing. The sorting process comes later. The more ideas you bring to light, the more choices you have. One idea leads to another.

Activity

Brainstorming is generally a group activity, but you can do it alone by using free association. Fill a page of your sketchbook/journal with words, jotting them down quickly and allowing each word to suggest the next. Start with a word that might be the subject of a picture. Write down words that describe, words that have a similar meaning, and words that mean the opposite—every word that comes to you. If a word slips in that has no apparent connection, write it down. Accept every word that comes. Sift through your list for unusual words to use with your subject. Sketch out ways you might relate these words to your subject in a picture.

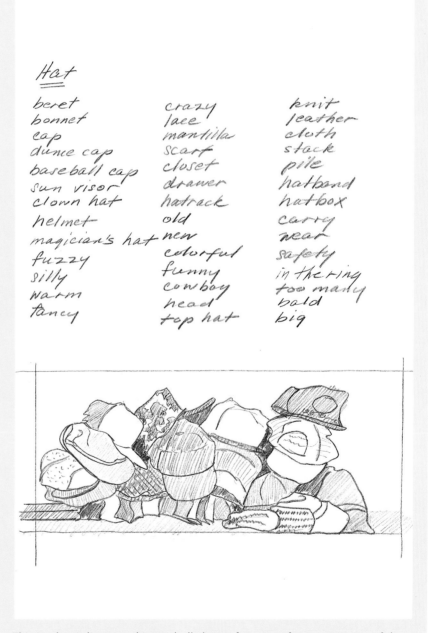

This is what I discovered in my hall closet after some free association of the word "hat"—a "found still life" ready and waiting to be turned into a picture.

Stop and Draw the Flowers

People tend to look at things without really seeing them. They block out the unfamiliar and allow access only to what they feel comfortable with. *Focus your awareness to discover things you have overlooked and things that others don't see.* This opens up a whole new world of sensations, a rich resource bank for creativity.

Examine a tree, a flower, a car, a stone, a building. Notice the smallest details. Look at it, touch it, smell it. Switch your attention to what you hear: birds singing, children laughing, a lawn mower buzzing. Did you hear them when you were using your eyes or did you "tune them in" only when you stopped to listen? Changing the focus of your sensual awareness is one of the keys to creativity. Like a zoom lens, your senses are focusing mechanisms. Train them to move around and refocus.

Look closely at sliced fruits and vegetables, noticing differences between the vertical and horizontal cuts in the same object. Notice the differences in rock formations along a cut in a mountain road and canyon walls shaped by moving water. Look at the patterns of buildings in the city. Visit a construction or a demolition site and look at cross sections of the buildings there. Pay attention to your surroundings. Practice memory drawing to sharpen your awareness of detail in the things you observe.

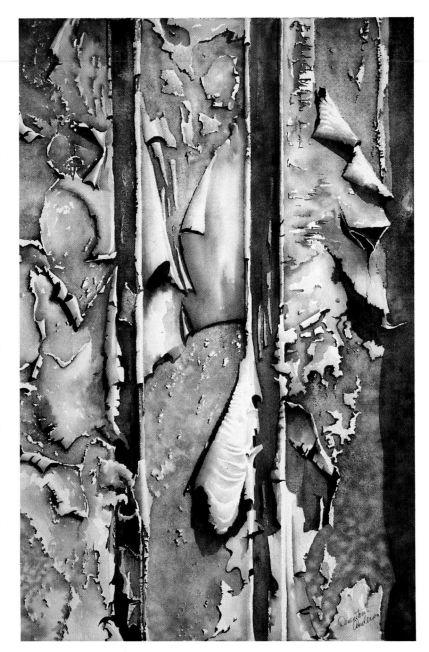

Would you have noticed the picture possibilities of a rusted, corrugated metal shed with paint peeling off it, or would you have walked on by, looking for a subject more "suitable" for art? This realistic rendering has strong abstract features. *Stars and Stripes Almost Forever* by Gayle Denington-Anderson. Watercolor, 23" x 16".

Activities

• Draw a sneaker, shoe, flower, teakettle, or camera from several points of view. Pick the object up and examine it closely. Feel its contours, note its hard and soft edges, look inside it, turn it upside down. You can do a more accurate drawing when you explore the object than you can just by looking at it. Draw the object on the same sheet from different angles as many times as you like. Look at every subject you choose this way, becoming familiar with it before you draw it.

• Look for images or designs in unexpected places. Slice a green pepper or a head of cabbage and draw the cross section. Transform this into drawings of landscapes, faces, figures, or abstract designs, dropping out some lines and adding others to strengthen the image. Use the natural pattern as a point of departure, then move any direction that suggests.

Explore and draw the things around you.

This cross section of a green pepper shows you how you can find raw designs in unexpected places.

These landscape and flower forms are derived from the cross section of the green pepper.

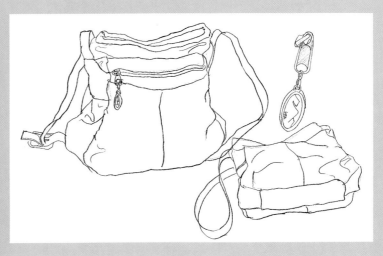

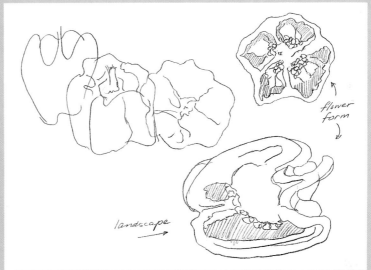

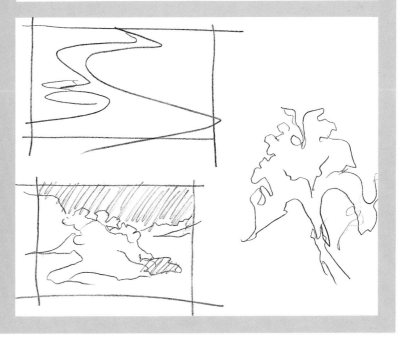

Take the High Road

Nothing is totally new. Your experiences and observations influence everything you paint or draw. You modify, add to, and subtract from what is there to make something new. However ordinary a subject may be, what you bring to it that is new is *yourself*. Your insights make it new again because your point of view is different from everybody else's. This is the real test of your emerging creativity—doing work that is neither repetitive of your previous work nor a copy of the work of others.

Tap your inner resources to find your responses to life's experiences. What makes you happy, sad, angry, calm? Your autobiographical collages draw upon this resource, and your artwork must do this, too. As an artist, you are more than an "eye." You are a heart and a mind. Reflect this in your art.

Your work should be your own. ***When you copy, you deny your uniqueness.*** Copying isn't creativity; it's just the "business of making a picture." When Peggie first came to my class, she had good watercolor skills, but had never painted an original picture. She was terrified to work from a real still life, but her first effort was more sensitive and personal than anything she had done before. Her work continues to reflect this sensitivity.

Art doesn't have to be shocking and outrageous to be original. Ben Shahn wrote in *The Shape of Content*:

> A work of art may rest its merits in traditional qualities; it may constitute a remarkable feat in craftsmanship; it may be a searching study into psychological states; it may be a hymn to nature; it may be a nostalgic glance backward; it may be any one of an infinite number of concepts, none of which may have any possible bearing upon its degree of newness.

Where do you find ideas? In familiar places such as supermarkets, libraries, malls, at the beach, at work, in the newspaper—try the classified section for a change!—at museums, galleries, and art fairs. In short: everywhere you go.

An elegantly dressed woman flanked by a beautiful home and surrounded by lovely objects is not an unusual subject for a painting. However, Melia's portrait of a lady is a highly original treatment, rich in color and texture. *Sunday Lady* by Paul Melia. Ink and gouache, 43" x 32".

Zampier's busy pen catches the pose of someone watching TV and says a little something about television itself. *Man Watching TV* by A. Brian Zampier, S.M. Pen and ink, 13 ½" x 10 ½".

In a more studied approach, Barrish records the big patterns, colors, and shapes. *Still Life* by A. Joseph Barrish, S.M. Markers, 12" x 9".

Detour Ahead

Sometimes you get stuck in the creative process and keep recycling the same ideas or abandoning work at the same unfinished state every time. The higher the stack of incomplete work, the more you avoid your studio!

Nearly everyone, from beginner to creative genius, experiences creative blocks. Many of these blocks are self-imposed. It takes time to make art, to develop skills, to nurture your creative spirit. The best way to deal with blocks is to *do something art-related every day,* no matter how small, to keep in touch with your creative self.

If you're squeezing your art in between watching a soap opera and reading a romance novel, adjust your priorities. Go to your art space and putter. File source material, sort out papers, sharpen pencils, stretch paper, test pigments. You might find a drawing or photo that suggests a possible subject. Even if you don't, you've still accomplished something related to your art.

Fifteen minutes of sketching while you're waiting for the car-pool or sitting in the doctor's office improves skills and weakens barriers to creativity.

When you have unfinished paintings piling up, don't think about the whole pile. Finish one. It feels good getting that piece out of your system and moving on to something new.

No picture is hopeless. You can always toss it in the collage box. But first, have some fun with it. Don't try to "save" the picture. Experiment with techniques and tools you've been afraid to use on something "good." Try some new tricks. Always be ready to move in a new direction.

Activity

Here's an easy way to get started in a new direction, using glue to get yourself unstuck. Make a mixture of 50 percent white polymer glue and 50 percent water. Glue rice paper or wrapping tissue on an old picture or one you haven't been able to finish. Let it dry, then paint into the new surface. The picture will have a totally different look. Layer background areas to suggest space or atmosphere; layer the foreground to enhance texture. Sprinkle sand or crumpled dry leaves in textured areas. You can learn something new from every experience with a picture.

This watercolor sketch needs an inventive touch to take it beyond the ordinary.

The sketch is transformed by the addition of a rice paper overlay that creates a whole new mood and texture.

Art in the Fast Lane

There will always be differences between artists' capabilities. People come to art from many different backgrounds: Some have been encouraged to cultivate art skills since they were children, so they pursue artistic interests freely. Others have been warned not to waste time in frivolous pursuits. They feel their artistic efforts are awkward and hopeless. You may have developed the habit of comparing yourself unfavorably with others. Don't do this to yourself! No two people progress at the same speed.

Some artists benefit from instruction in classes and exchange of ideas in art groups. Others are better off working on their own, using books of self-instruction like this one to help them develop skills and explore new ideas. You are likely to develop a more personal art when you work independently, uninfluenced by fads and frills in techniques.

Have reasonable expectations about what it will take— and how long it will take—to reach your goals. Compare your work only with what you have done before and not with the work of other artists.

You improve a little bit each time you paint or draw. Give yourself many opportunities to do these things. Start with materials at hand—pencil, pen, or crayon and paper. One day you will be astonished that you ever thought you were not creative.

Have fun with your art. Maybe you are trying too hard to please others. Now is the time to please yourself. Approach your art playfully and not for the approval of other people. Tune out criticism. Persevere in what you are doing regardless of comments from others. I believe in you. Believe in yourself.

Maybe you are overly concerned with selling your work or getting into shows. In *Fire in the Crucible*, John Briggs relates that people involved in creative tasks work harder and are more absorbed in their work when they are doing it for their own satisfaction. When they are offered a reward, they become less creative and do only what they have to do to get the reward.

Creativity is its own reward!

In a more or less realistically rendered scene, the artist has suspended motion and time, making the picture both whimsical and mysterious. Clearly, Barnum enjoys making his art, and his delight, in turn, brings pleasure to his viewers. This is largely what creativity is all about! *Boogie Boards* by Robert L. Barnum. Watercolor, 21" x 15".

Different Directions

The desire to change and grow is a manifestation of creativity. People who are dissatisfied with current achievements or are restless to move into new territory are ripe for creative change. This is what prompts a non-artist to venture into the realm of art or causes an accomplished artist to switch to a different medium or style.

How can you, as an artist, improve your artistic skills at your present level or break through to the next level? *Change!* How can you get more in touch with your creative self? *Change!*

Change and risk-taking are normal aspects of the creative process. They are the lubricants that keep the wheels in motion. A creative act is not necessarily something that has *never* been done; it is something *you* have never done. Every day, try something *you* haven't done before. As anthropologist Margaret Mead said,

To the extent a person makes, invents or thinks something that is new to him, he may be said to have performed a creative act.

Build the courage to try new things. Would you like to learn to paint a watercolor or paint a mural on a building? Do you want to take a class at the YMCA or go to art school in New York? Take a workshop in Alaska? Exhibit in a national show? Go for it! A change in direction—even a small one—fosters creativity. *You never know what you can do until you try.*

Access your creativity by looking for alternatives to everything you think and do about art. Search for possibilities, not just the habitual or the obvious. Mix mediums, find an unusual viewpoint, use ordinary tools in extraordinary ways, juxtapose bits and pieces of unrelated objects and ideas to create new forms or ideas. There are many answers to a

Melia's boats suggest different levels of reality, including what is seen and what is imagined in the same picture. *Déjà Vu* by Paul Melia. Pen and ink, gouache and acrylic, 30" by 40".

question; there are many solutions to a problem. You find them by looking for them!

You can see on these pages how three artists approach the subject of boats, using different mediums and techniques. How many ways can *you* think of to paint boats? On the water, at the dock, in dry dock, beached, in a storm, becalmed, in the sky, upside down in the grass, with people in them, with animals (Noah's ark?), with cargo, sailing, cruising, racing, towing, tugging. What if you changed your medium? The center of interest? The shape of the support? What if you made a cubist or an abstract boat? Or turned the boat into a watermelon sailing on a sea of cranberry punch?

This sketchbook notation records information for future reference. What Barrish sees in the harbor is different from what you might see. *Harbor Scene, Boothbay, Maine* by A. Joseph Barrish, S.M. Markers, 12" x 9".

• HARBOR SCENE
BOOTHBAY • MAINE •

Here is still another way of looking at boats. Good design and solid technique are the strong points in Sovek's painting. *Marina* by Charles Sovek. Oil on canvas, 20" x 24". Private collection.

One of a series based on aspects of the game of chess and the game of life, this painting is structured with several limitations: 64 squares — each is different, yet contains similar elements or connects in some way with other squares; and a limited palette. Each square is a composition in itself, as are various groupings of squares. By staying within these parameters, Barnes does a lot of focused, creative problem solving. *64 Squares* by Curtis Barnes. Oil on canvas, 32″ x 32″.

You're on Your Way

Rollo May, in *The Courage to Create*, wrote:

> *Creativity . . . requires limits, for the creative act arises out of the struggle of human beings with and against that which limits them.*

When you decide on your medium, choose a subject, or select a color scheme, you are setting boundaries for your creative energy. You have

great freedom within this framework. Without such limits, however, everything is chaos. Limitations focus your creativity. These limits are the basis for the challenge that makes artmaking an exciting and satisfying pursuit.

Are you still concerned about talent? Many definitions of creativity exclude talent as a prerequisite to art, placing emphasis on desire, perseverance, determination. In short, it takes self-discipline. Sidney Harris, a newspaper columnist, wrote:

Self-discipline without talent can often achieve astounding results, whereas talent without self-discipline inevitably dooms itself to failure.

Creativity is not a magical ingredient of personality granted to a chosen few. Creativity is an attitude you hold toward the choices that you make in life, as well as in art. There is always a better way of doing things and creative people are out there looking for it!

It isn't drudgery. ***Creativity is fun and life-enhancing!*** When you combine playfulness and a spirit of adventure with discipline and self-control, you experience the true joy of being a creative person.

Do you think this beautiful painting would have seen the light of day without tremendous dedication and self-discipline? It takes more than a good beginning to have a successful finish. *Taos Tapestry* by Juanita Williams. Watercolor and gouache, 40″ x 60″. Collection of the artist.

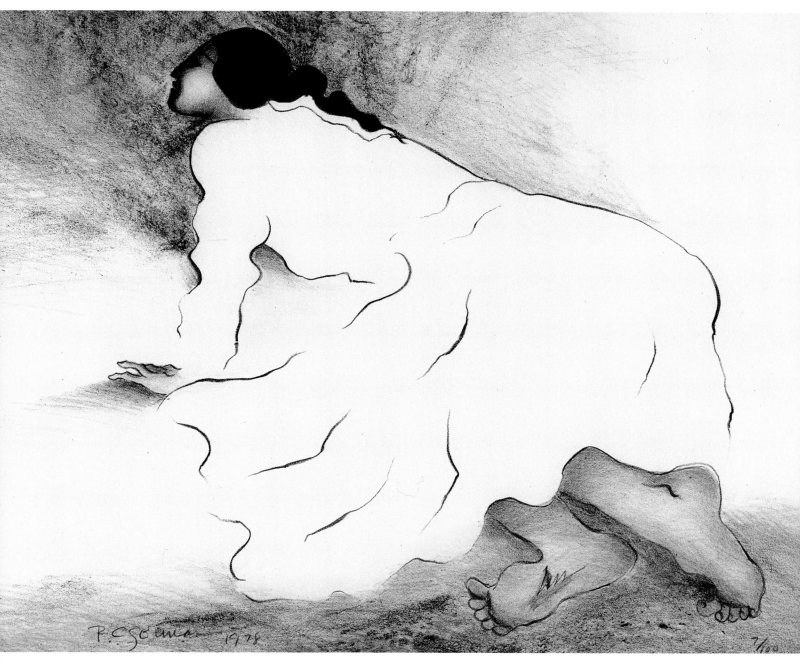

Gorman uses a limited number of lines to suggest contour, mass, and movement all at the same time. The line is both earthy and elegant as it describes the shape and mood of Changing Woman, a subject of Navajo mythology, whose image is the most persistent of Gorman's themes. *Barefoot Lady* by R. C. Gorman. Lithograph, 12″ x 15″.

Chapter 2

Drawing: Don't Leave Home Without It

"You are not copying nature, but responding to nature in full awareness, to the way nature expresses itself in that object."

Frederick Franck, The Zen of Seeing/Drawing

Many years of continual drawing for work and pleasure have made it possible for this artist to create a quick sketch that is both well-composed and accurate in its representation of the subject. Melia is a careful draftsman. Each scribbled line is preceded by a moment of sharp observation and mental calculation, then recorded by his well-trained hand. *Seagulls* by Paul Melia. Pen and ink, 8 ½" x 11".

What vehicle is the most reliable means to carry you on your venture into creativity?

Drawing!

Drawing is the foundation of art. This chapter is not about how to draw, but how to enjoy the creative experience of drawing so you will draw more and build a stronger base for your art. With a little less emphasis on "results," drawing can be a lot more enjoyable. Drawing requires no exceptional ability—only normal vision and a degree of coordination. You instinctively know how to draw.

If you feel drawing isn't your strong suit, this chapter will help you gain confidence. If you already draw with assurance, it will help you develop more individuality and creativity in your drawing.

You gain many important benefits when you draw. First, ***drawing stimulates your natural curiosity.*** Creative people ask lots of questions, so anything that encourages you to do this enhances your creativity. Second, ***drawing forces you to observe objects carefully***, so you learn to see accurately. Third, ***every time you draw you improve your eye-to-hand coordination.*** Skills improve naturally with practice. Finally, ***when you draw, you think like an artist.***

As you draw, you gather information about how things work, how the pieces fit together. You gain insight into nature's laws: how a stream creates its meandering path, how the wind twists trees, how a leaf mimics a tree. You find and record relationships. Drawing provides a sort of subconscious warehouse of resources for creative imagery, and your job is to fill the warehouse.

In a drawing you define something you cannot quite describe in words. You reveal your visual experience in a unique way, by your touch with tools and materials.

You learn about yourself when you draw: the power of your motivation, concentration, and endurance. You develop self-confidence.

Activity

Pick a drawing from this book or use an editorial cartoon or magazine illustration. Make a viewfinder from a piece of heavy paper with an opening that is one-inch square. Place it over a small area of the drawing. Copy the marks inside the viewfinder in a square in your sketchbook. Notice the quality of line, estimate the pressure and speed of the mark, and emulate these in your drawing. Change tools and make another drawing. Observe how the lines made by a different tool alter the character of the drawing. You can control the expression in a drawing by using different tools and adjusting your "touch" to them.

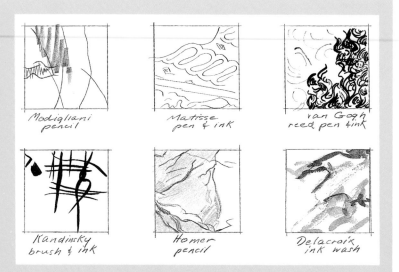

These viewfinder drawings are based on drawings by masters.

Your Tool Kit

I'll bet there are a lot of art materials you haven't explored. Now's the time! Explore anything that makes a mark and every surface that accepts a mark. Change materials frequently. Use different combinations of tools and surfaces.

Try these: pencils, graphite sticks, charcoal, markers, wax crayons, colored pencils, pastels, oil pastels, conté crayons, ordinary chalk. Try a ballpoint pen, a steel nib pen, a sliver of bamboo or a stick dipped in ink, a brush dipped in watercolor. Make marks with food coloring and a toothpick, eye shadow and an applicator, shoe polish and a cotton swab. Find five more tools around the house that make marks and experiment with them.

Make marks on drawing paper, newspapers, typing paper, crumpled paper bags, freezer paper, wrapping tissue, paper towels, charcoal or pastel paper, rice paper, watercolor paper, corrugated cardboard, illustration board, pebble mat board. Draw on wet and dry paper. Find five more surfaces you can make marks on and try them.

In the simplest terms, drawing is making marks on a surface. Everyone has a unique "touch" with a tool: a different speed or pressure, a distinctive gesture or stroke. Creative drawing capitalizes on your unique way of making marks—your personal touch.

You make two marks when you draw: a dot and a line. What could be easier? There is no "right" way to make the marks. They can be sharp and decisive or soft and fuzzy; nervous and agitated or placid and even-handed. Do whatever feels natural to you and you will put your personal imprint indelibly in your drawing. *Your drawing is always a reflection of yourself.*

Here's a sampling of marks and tools. What else can you find around the house that can be used as a drawing tool?

Drawing animals from life calls for a quick assessment of proportions, rapid recording of marks, and a suggestion of significant detail. Stolzenberger accomplishes all of this with an unlabored line that quickly suggests the character of the animal. *Pig* by Sharon L. Stolzenberger. Charcoal, 12" x 17 ½".

BOOTHBAY
HARBOR M·A·IN·E

Barrish makes his on-site sketches with an altogether different type of mark. The difference is a result of the medium used and the artist's individual style. Don't forget to figure in the type of subject when deciding on an approach. The landscape permits a careful design, while a living animal is a moving target, calling for a quick sketch. *Boothbay Harbor, Maine* by A. Joseph Barrish, S.M. Markers, 12" x 9".

Drawing **29**

Activities

• In your sketchbook/journal draw two or three six-inch squares. Make dots, lines, and areas in the squares. Begin with the familiar pencil. Vary the pressure on the pencil, turn it this way and that, move it across the paper at different speeds, jab it into the page. See how many different kinds of line one implement will make. Close your eyes as you move the pencil over the paper. Sense the resistance of the surface. Try a smooth sheet of typing paper, then a textured sheet of charcoal or pastel paper.

• Experiment with blending in another square. Smudge the marks with your finger, rub with a cotton swab. Make a shaded area by placing dots and lines close together and smudging the marks with your thumb. Do you like the shading or do you favor a crisp, linear look?

• Change to a ballpoint pen, a marker, or a piece of charcoal, and fill a square with marks. Compare these marks with the pencil marks. Which do you like better: sensuous, flowing marks or rough-and-tumble marks? A free, gestural stroke or a tightly controlled mark? Delicate pencil marks or bold marker lines? Describe your marks. They have a character of their own, determined by the tools you use and your manner of handling them. This eventually develops into a style as your preferences for certain tools and your unique way of working come to the surface.

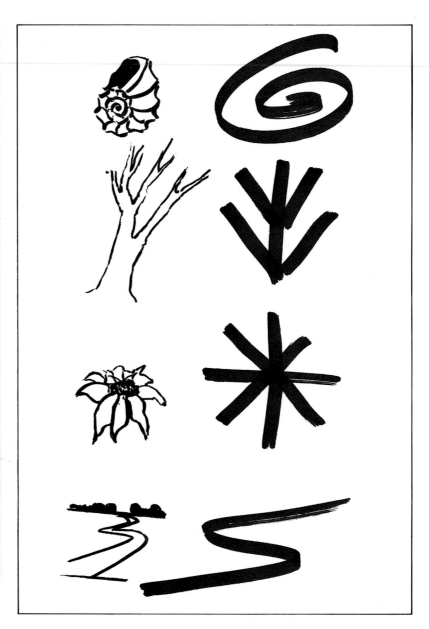

Look for these natural patterns in your subjects.

Classic Lines

Random marks don't make a picture. Dots and lines have to be organized to be effective. One way to combine dots and lines is according to basic patterns found in nature. Man-made and natural objects all have structural integrity and dynamic energy that can be used to strengthen and animate your drawing and make it more creative. Look for a pattern, then make marks that emphasize this underlying design.

The *spiral* pattern is seen in many seashells, vining plants, whirlpools, and tornadoes. The spiral line coils around itself without reconnecting.

The *branching* pattern is found in trees and leaves, with lines radiating from a central trunk. The tributaries of a river and the human circulatory system are other examples.

In the *radial* pattern, lines radiate from or converge on a center. Look at a spider web, a daisy, a starfish.

A *meandering* line twists and doubles back toward itself, as you can see in the carving of a streambed by water.

There is no "correct" line in art. The patterns and lines of nature can be simplified, expanded, or combined. Your representation of this may be bold and direct or delicate and sensitive.

When we make drawings with our eyes closed or doodle absent-mindedly, quite often natural patterns, such as the spiral found in this picture, appear spontaneously. Fortener has developed the image and its symbolism into a drawing that at the same time is deeply meaningful to her and is visually pleasing to the viewer. *Deep Down Things* by Sue Fortener. Colored pencil on handmade paper, 30" diameter.

Routine Maintenance

You can draw, even if you think you can't. You can improve, even if you're stuck. And you can benefit from drawing, even if you don't make realistic art. Drawing carries you to your artistic destination. *Establish and maintain a drawing habit.*

Drawing is a mechanical skill that improves with practice. If you really want to draw well, you can do it—by doing it.

A working artist knows that drawing strengthens observation skills and manual dexterity. What some think is a talent for drawing is a skill that has been highly developed through exercise. Every drawing experience is an opportunity for you to improve these skills. You develop the conviction that you *can* draw, that you don't have to prove or apologize for your drawing skills.

Confidence in your drawing skills enables you to be more daring in experimental work.

Reinforce the drawing habit. Draw something—anything—every day. Keep a pencil and paper by the phone, in the family room, in the kitchen, and in the car. Doodle while you're on the phone: draw the phone, the dial, and the cord. Draw odds and ends: a pop can, bone, pencil sharpener, tea-kettle, or geranium plant. Draw from memory and imagination: an apple orchard, the neighbor's dog, a man-eating flower, a frog who is a prince, a martian.

Draw with your right hand, then with your left, with your eyes open or closed. Whenever you see a pencil, pick it up and draw. *You learn to draw by drawing!*

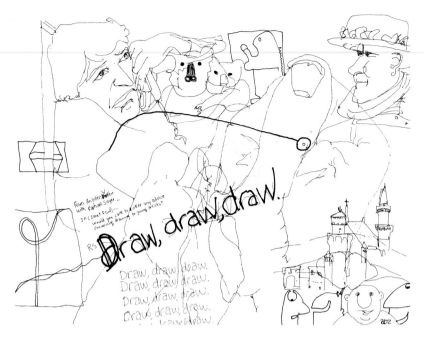

What more can I say? *Draw, Draw, Draw* by A. Brian Zampier, S.M. Pen and ink, 9″ x 12″.

Melia feels compelled to draw just about everything he sees, so he has developed the capability to make a telling statement every time he puts pencil or pen to paper. You shouldn't worry about who is watching or even whether the drawing will turn out. Your main concern should be simply to draw. *French Riviera* by Paul Melia. Colored pencil, 10″ x 14″.

Activity

Turn on the TV and sketch a news-person, an announcer, or a weather forecaster—someone who doesn't move around a lot. Make a few simple lines for the head and shoulders and just a suggestion of features. Switch to a sports event and scribble some drawings to capture the action. Note that certain poses and movements are repeated frequently, for example, the setup of a football lineman or a tennis player's serve. Start your drawing, then wait until the same pose is taken to carry it further. When you sketch, don't be concerned about making a finished drawing. Draw for the fun of it. Draw often and your skills will rapidly improve.

Figure Skaters by A. Brian Zampier, S.M. Pen and ink, 13 ½" x 10 ½".

Watching the News by A. Brian Zampier, S.M. Pen and ink, 7 ¾" x 10 ½".

Getting the Wheels Turning

Drawing helps you to see and seeing helps you to draw. You think that when your eyes are open you are seeing, but your brain plays tricks on you, reporting stereotypes instead of what your eyes actually see. It gives you a quick and easy symbol—the tree looks like a lollipop, the eye looks like an almond—so it won't have to work so hard searching for individual differences.

Studies in "right brain drawing" by Dr. Betty Edwards suggest that most people see and draw more accurately when they shut down the time-oriented, verbal left side of the brain and allow the space-oriented, intuitive right side to function more freely.

You do this by confusing the left brain. One way is to change the labels. Don't call what you're drawing by name; think of it as "a curved line about so long" or "a space this high and that wide."

You might also draw a picture upside down. Place a drawing upside down beside your paper. Start at the top of your page and follow each line, moving slowly from one line to the next. Frequently check the size of the spaces between lines, the angles and directions of each line, and their distance from the edges of the paper. Frustrate the efficient left brain by concentrating and working slowly and intently.

In class Suzy was ready to give up on her drawing of a swan floating on a quiet pond. She had the reflection just right, but couldn't get the swan. So she flipped her reference photo and her picture and drew a perfect swan upside down.

Use all of your senses to discover the essence of every object you draw—especially objects you see every day.

Some draw as a mystical experience, entering into a silent, internal dialogue with the object, searching for its special qualities, seeing it as if nothing else exists at that moment. Frederick Franck, artist and philosopher, wrote in *The Zen of Seeing/Drawing:*

I have learned that what I have not drawn I have never really seen, and that when I start drawing an ordinary thing I realize how extraordinary it is, sheer miracle. . . .

Place a simple object on a table: a shell, a leaf, a weed, an acorn, a twig. What do you see? Is it worn or broken? What forces of nature have affected it? How is it unique from others of its kind?

Slowly draw what you see, sensing the meaning of what you are looking at. Make your dots and lines express fragility or the enduring quality of the object.

See it! Draw it!

Improve your ability to see by touching, smelling, tasting, and listening as well as looking. Use all of your senses to "experience" the object in several different ways. Your perception is sharper with unfamiliar objects or things that have been changed. Find an object around the house, office, or garage: a power drill, an ice skate, a leaf blower, a meat grinder. Place it on a table and study it. Does it have a cord or a handle? How many eyelets for the laces? What kind of blade does it have? Is it sharp? Heavy? Pick the object up and examine it. Feel it, smell it, shake it. Does it rattle? Ask yourself: How is it constructed? How do the pieces fit together? What makes it work? Look for basic shapes and notice how they are connected. Details are simply decoration on the surface of these shapes: circles, triangles, and rectangles. Start with an analysis of simple shapes. Find larger shapes first, then fit the smaller shapes into them.

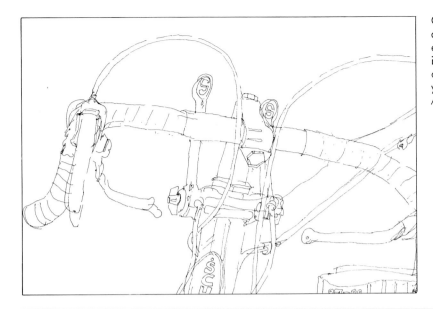

Concentrate on one section of a complicated object rather than the entire thing, and you'll find interesting compositions like this one. Work out the relationships of parts before you tackle the whole. *My Bike* by A. Brian Zampier, S.M. Pen and ink, 9" x 12".

Activities

• Make a line drawing upside down. Use the drawing shown here or a cartoon. Outline a frame on your paper. Work slowly from the top down, connecting shapes as you would attach pieces to a jigsaw puzzle.

• Ask a friend to place an object in a paper bag without showing it to you. Reach into the bag without looking and then draw the object using only your sense of touch.

Drawing something upside down helps you turn off the logical, analytical part of your brain, so the creative part can take over. *Bill.*

A Guided Tour of Drawing Methods

A drawing "method" is just another way of making marks. Artists use controlled lines, free lines, or a combination of both. *Contour, gesture*, and *tonal* drawing are the basic methods. In *Experimental Drawing*, artist Robert Kaupelis writes:

> *It is my firm belief that contour, gesture, and modeled drawing are absolutely fundamental modes of working for all artists. . . . No artist that I know ever stops using these modes of drawing.*

Contour Drawing

A contour drawing differs from an outline. A contour line describes three-dimensional form, moving into and across an object to indicate volume. An outline follows only the outer boundaries. Concentration, careful observation, and slow, coordinated movement of the eye and hand are essential to contour drawing.

In *pure contour drawing* you trace contours without looking at your drawing paper, which is taped to the table top. Sit so you can see the object you are drawing, but not the paper. Begin anywhere, slowly moving your pencil as though it were attached to your eye as it moves around the object. Concentrate. Distortion in contour drawings is caused by moving your eye and hand at different rates of speed or by losing your concentration.

Controlled contour drawing allows you to peek at the paper occasionally to check on the location or direction of your pencil. *Quick contour* is a rapid gestural line that captures only the most essential contour lines.

This lightly shaded drawing shows how the contour line suggests weight and mass, as opposed to the flat appearance of a simple outline. *Contour Figure Drawing* by Elaine Szelestey. Pencil, 15" x 9".

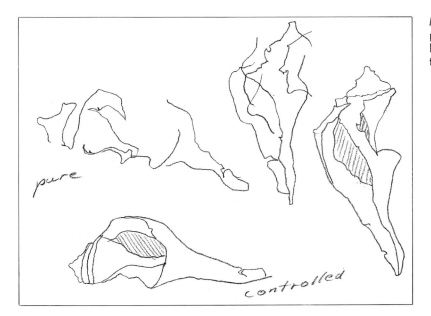

Making contour drawings like this pencil drawing of a broken shell can help develop eye-hand coordination.

Activities

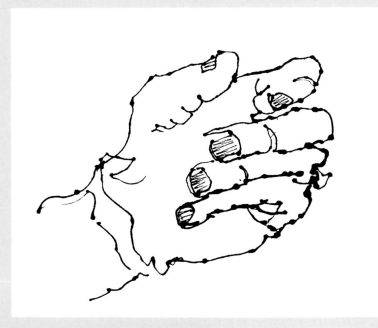

Make a contour drawing of your own hand.

Concentrate on both contour and gesture as you draw with your eyes closed.

• Some of the most interesting drawings in an artist's sketchbook are of the artist's own hand—the most readily available model you can find! Do a contour drawing of your hand with felt-tip pen and absorbent paper, such as wrapping tissue or rice paper. Keep the pen in contact with the paper at all times. It will track the starts and stops in the line as you pause to look and then continue drawing.

• Make a pure contour drawing and a controlled contour drawing of any object within reach, following the directions in the text. Next, concentrate on the same object for two or three minutes, then close your eyes, and draw its gesture. When you draw, think about both contour and gesture of your subject and consider which aspect would be most expressive in your drawing.

A gesture drawing isn't a "finished" drawing, so capture a gesture quickly and do many sketches from quick poses. If the model doesn't move, then change your position for a different view of the gesture. *Studies from Life* by Elaine Szelestey. Pencil, 14" x 17".

Using a brush with watercolor or ink forces you to make a few bold strokes to record the gesture without "noodling" unnecessary detail. Use a big brush for this and your gestural drawing will suggest a remarkable sense of form as well as gesture. *Study* by Elaine Szelestey. Watercolor, 14" x 11".

Gesture Drawing

Gesture drawing catches the gesture of the subject: not what it looks like, but what it is doing. Capture this by "feeling the pose," letting it flow outward through your pencil onto the paper.

Gesture lines put energy into the drawing—the fluid grace of a ballerina or the frantic pedaling of a bicycle racer. Look for the gesture before you begin to draw.

Everything has gesture: a cowboy boot, an alley cat, a Volkswagen, a tulip, and a Shaker chair.

Minimize detail in gesture drawing. Reveal the life force beneath the surface of the object. Interpret your subject's gesture through your own gestures, making firm, hard strokes or using light, delicate marks where needed. Your drawing can be even more expressive if you exaggerate or distort the gesture.

Take your sketchbook and pencil or markers to the shopping mall. Draw the gestures of passers-by. Draw children on a playground. Draw the people on your TV screen. Draw a plate of spaghetti.

In a series of several drawings, Marcus noted her daughter's changing gestures as she sat immersed in the book she was reading. Each drawing immediately communicates to the viewer the girl's gesture at that moment. *Girl Reading* by Joan Marcus. Pencil, 14″ x 11″.

Stage 1: The circular format is established and random lines are quickly scribbled into it with graphite pencil. Rubbings, templates, patterns, erasures are all rapidly set down without a thought to organization. *Developing a Mandala* by Ardis Macaulay. Graphite and colored pencil, 12" x 12".

Stage 2: This mandala has been unified with tones and highlights into a cohesive design. It can be developed further if the artist is so inclined.

Alternative to Stage 2: Colored pencil was used to complete this mandala
after the automatic drawing stage in graphite.

If there is a life drawing group any-where in town, you'll find Elaine Szelestey there, hard at work draw-ing gestures and contours of figures as well as portraits in every conceiv-able medium. Her dedication has paid off in the ability to make an expressive drawing of even the most ordinary pose. *Seated Figure* by Elaine Szelestey. Oil pastel, 22 1/2" x 15".

In this meticulously rendered draw-ing, you can see it is possible to sug-gest line without actually drawing lines and to denote tone without smudging. The trick is to accomplish a striking, carefully crafted drawing that isn't stiff and overworked. Price is successful here. *Ashley* by Charles K. Price. Pen and ink, 20" x 26".

Faces and Figures

You can draw the human fig-ure. If you can draw an egg, you can draw a leg. Like all drawing, it takes careful obser-vation of contour, gesture, and tone—and some practice. You will improve every time you draw. Study the gallery of fig-ures and portraits on these pages to see how experienced artists approach these subjects.

Don't be embarrassed to draw from live models. Draw from life at every opportunity, whether nude models or clothed ones. Join a life draw-ing group or form your own group. Gather together a group of artist friends and take turns drawing each other. Bring interesting accessories— floppy brim hats, scarves, clunky jewelry, pipes, eye-glasses—to make it more inter-esting. Set a time limit for each

model, no more than thirty minutes. Begin with five minutes of gesture drawing—thirty-second poses. Next, ten minutes of contour drawing of any part of the face or figure. Finish with fifteen minutes of tonal drawing.

Then work with another model and a different drawing mode: caricature. Exaggerate features and proportions to create a lofty expression, making the highbrow higher or the innocent eyes even wider. A group of four to six artists can get a lot of drawing experience and have a good time while doing it. I hope you're still friends after the caricatures, though!

Draw the kids as they watch TV, shoppers at the mall, your neighbor working in the yard. You will become accustomed to drawing in public and drawing real people—if you do it often. Practice will teach you what makes a drawing of a face or figure convincing and expressive. Almost any medium can be used for figure or portrait drawing. The drawing may be a quick gestural sketch or a finely crafted rendering.

Visiting family in the Northwest, Szelestey found a subject new to her: native Americans. Her exploratory drawings and paintings now frequently reflect this new interest. *An American Indian* by Elaine Szelestey. Graphite, 17" x 14".

Tinkelman's treatment of a native American subject is quite different from Szelestey's. As he shows here, movement can be indicated by the overall design, pose, and placement of the figure without reliance on gestural marks or contour lines. *Hoop Dancer* by Murray Tinkelman. Pen and inks, 20" x 16".

Lacking a model, Szelestey threw some sketches on the floor and painted them with a strong light and shadow pattern, a creative and eye-catching approach. The effect is so convincing that a judge in a watercolor show asked the committee to move the painting out of the strong light so she could examine it. (*Sketches* won an award!) *Sketches* by Elaine Szelestey. Watercolor, 30" x 40".

Activity

The lack of a model shouldn't prevent you from drawing faces. You can always be your own model. If you have never done a self portrait, now's the time to do it. Set up a medium-sized cosmetic mirror as near eye level as possible. Make a contour drawing of your reflection. Move the mirror high or low for a distorted angle.

Make faces at yourself in the mirror and do gesture drawings of your facial expressions in pencil or marker.

You always have one model handy—yourself! Make faces at yourself to practice capturing expressions.

Ouch!

Sketching

The sketch hunter moves through life as he finds it, not passing negligently the things he loves, but stopping to know them, and to note them down in the shorthand of his sketchbook. . . .
Robert Henri, The Art Spirit

Sketching is the note-taking of drawing. You don't need the details, just a reminder. Mistakes don't count! With a few quick strokes, note the essential information from your observation, a partial statement.

Sketching allows you to explore and enjoy the things that interest and amuse you. Keep a sketchbook in the car; take it to the beach. Sketch a little every day and in no time, you will find substantial improvement in your skills and greater confidence in your drawing.

If you only have time for a quick, on-the-spot notation, get it down and you can check the perspective later! To record a detail for future reference, make a careful contour drawing.

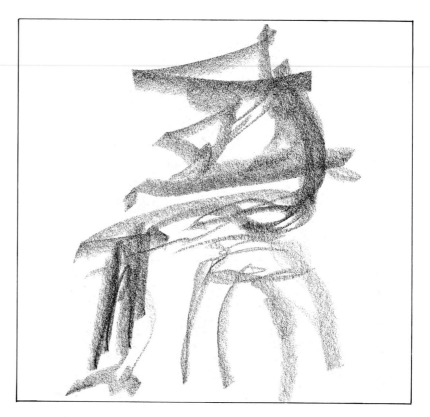

A gestural sketch. Quick! Before she leaves! Woman in a chair. Pencil, 9″ x 12″.

Melia's main interest here was the pattern, although volume certainly plays a big part in his sketch. *Woman in A Chair* by Paul Melia. Pen and ink, 8 ½″ x 11″.

This quick notation of color and patterns at a vacation "watering hole" could easily serve as the reference for a full-scale painting. But don't make that your reason for sketching—sketch for no reason at all! You'll enjoy it more that way. *Raw Bar* by Sharon L. Stolzenberger. Charcoal pencil and watercolor, 12" x 18".

Activity

My students often have difficulty finding subject matter for drawing and painting, usually because they have a tendency to overlook the potential of things that are familiar. This activity will help you to seek out subject matter and will also give you additional sketching experience. Make twenty-six 3" x 4" rectangles in your sketchbook. Mark each space with a letter of the alphabet from A to Z. Then start a sketcher's scavenger hunt: find a subject in your home or office, inside or outside, beginning with each letter. Sketch it in the appropriate box, using markers, ballpoint pen, sketching pen, pencil, or colored pencil. Allow yourself a week to finish the alphabet. (A big pat on the back if you find an X, Y, and Z!)

Go on a sketcher's scavenger hunt.

Looking up instead of down, Vanderbeek takes advantage of an unusual viewpoint to exaggerate and distort for dramatic effect. *Banker* by Don Vanderbeek. Watercolor and pastel, 15" x 20".

Zampier does a great many drawings of what he sees, then his imagination goes wild and funny people and animals begin to populate the pictures. Don't try to make your drawings "precious objects." Have fun while you're learning and don't stop playing just because you feel you are improving. *Funny Faces* by A. Brian Zampier, S.M. Pen and ink with watercolor, 14" x 10 ½".

Look for a New Angle

If good drawing is essentially a matter of careful observation and skillful recording, then how can drawing be creative? Because your drawing has your touch in it. You can pick a subject that is special to you. You can rearrange what you're looking at any way you like. And you can do anything that will make it fun!

You can change mediums, reverse values, devise an unusual color scheme. You can distort and exaggerate, draw what you feel instead of what you see. Knowing that you can draw correctly if you want to gives you the confidence to experiment.

Look at a subject from different viewpoints. From directly above (the *bird's eye view*), you see shapes and relationships that are entirely different from the normal view. The *ant's-eye view*—looking up from floor level—distorts the image.

This angle gives the viewer a feeling of floating over the subject. It takes a good grasp of perspective and sharp observation to do this as effectively as Vanderbeek. *Neon Movies* by Don Vanderbeek. Pastel, 20" x 15".

Activities

• Use a checkerboard grid to stretch, compress, or distort a picture. First, draw a grid on a photograph or drawing. Then draw another grid with the same number of lines on a sheet of paper, altering the sizes and shapes of the sections in the grid. Distort the entire grid or only parts of it. Transfer your picture to the distorted grid, copying the marks in one section of the original onto the corresponding section of the distorted grid, changing them as needed to accommodate the different shape.

• Do gestural sketches of yourself or someone else with black marker, exaggerating facial expressions and features.

Exaggerated facial expressions can have dramatic or amusing effects.

Use a grid to distort your subject.

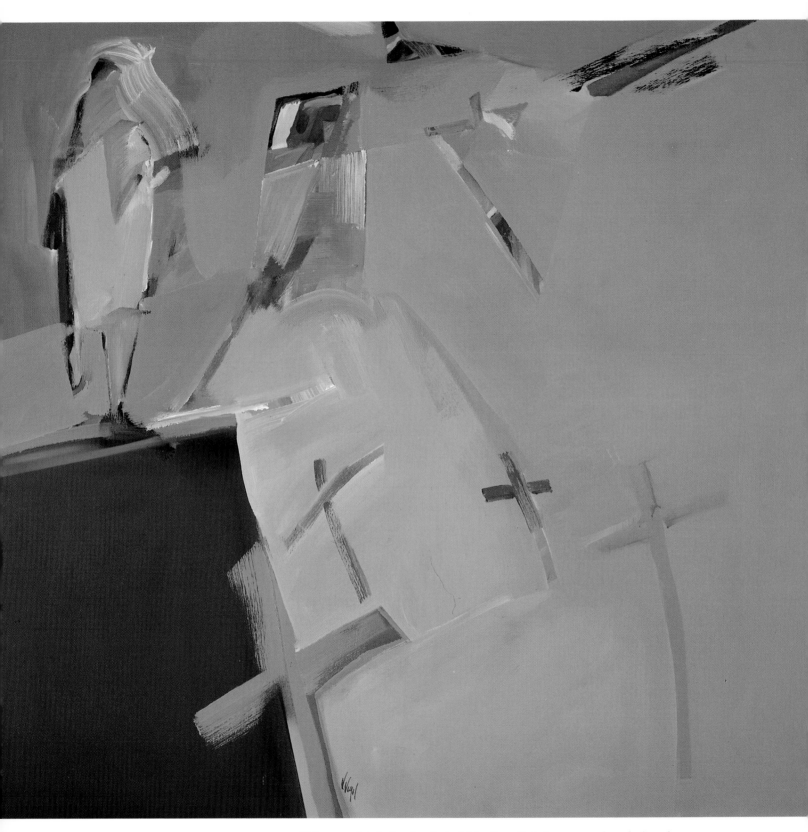

This powerful abstraction includes both realistic images and symbolic references unified by strong color and shape relationships. The design expresses movement, ambiguous space, and a sense of mystery. *Lomita Rosa* by Veloy Vigil. Acrylic on canvas, 48" x 48".

Chapter 3
Design: Mapping Your Route

You have decided on your destination, packed your bags, and put your vehicle in good shape for your creative journey. Wouldn't you like to take off right now? I know the feeling! But you're not quite ready yet. You need to map the route, become familiar with the major highways, and learn the rules of the road before you start off.

Can you find your way without looking at the map? Of course. You might even make some lucky discoveries as you go, but you could also get hopelessly lost. It's better to plan the trip, so you can choose alternate routes as you go without losing your general sense of direction.

Making art is more than exercising technical skill with materials. The work of art is the synthesis of *what you see* (sensation), *what you feel* (emotion), and *what you understand* (comprehension). These three things interact, guided by knowledge stored in your unconscious. They are focused on one objective: to turn raw ma-

Shunk begins by transferring old magazine pictures to rag paper, then uses color areas and gestural marks to tie the images together and create tension on the picture surface. He selects the images at random but unifies the picture through the force of design.
Timepiece by Hal Shunk. Transfer drawing and pastel, 29 ½" x 21 ½".

Melia's painting is like a tapestry, rich with color. Images relevant to the idea he is communicating are woven throughout, arranged to create a point of light here, a necessary dark accent there. *Great American Dream* by Paul Melia. Transparent inks, 29" x 37".

terials and technical skills into a work of art.

How do you bring all these factors together?

Design!

Design turns nature into art. What you see in the world around you may be interesting, beautiful, challenging, or frightening, but it isn't art until you shape it into a painting or drawing. Flowers. A bag lady. A sunset. A snake. Anger. Joy. As an artist, you mold these raw materials into art through the use of design, simplifying the complex, organizing the cluttered world into a coherent, meaningful image that expresses a concept.

Art is a visual language: Drawing is the vocabulary and design principles are the rules of grammar. Once you have a firm grasp on these fundamentals, using them becomes second nature, just like writing and speaking.

You are a designer already. You make design decisions ev-

ery day when you select clothing, buy a car, arrange the dinner table, move the furniture in your office. Paying attention and caring about how you do these things enables you to do them more creatively. The more creative you are in your daily life, the more creative you will be in your art.

Why Design?

Design is the road map, the blueprint, the organization of your picture. Design may be simple or complex — three miles to the grocery or a trip around the world, a simple drawing or a monumental mural. Design is the human mind at work, selecting, simplifying, embellishing, making choices that reveal the artist's personality, perceptions, and insights.

Design is problem solving: the arrangement of shapes, values and colors on a two-dimensional surface; the division of space and placement of major forms. The formal elements of design are found in every good picture, whether realistic or abstract.

Each design decision reinforces the expressive idea you wish to communicate. It isn't the object that you paint or draw that communicates with the viewer; it's how you present it that counts. When you paint power and energy use strong diagonals, hard edges, bold brush strokes to help convey those ideas. For sensitivity use soft edges, close values, delicate color.

Design directs the viewer's eye through the picture. Ed Whitney said, "Invite your viewer into the picture and entertain him everywhere." You set the pace, determine the directional flow. Your eye path leads to exciting key areas, through restful quiet passages, moving in and around your center of interest. You accomplish this through relationships of shapes, continuity of line, color concept, interaction with the edges of the support, and manipulation of space. The elements and principles of design help you to do this.

What happens to creativity if you place so much emphasis on formal design? Do rules and organization interfere with having fun and letting yourself go? Not at all. As we saw in Chapter One, creativity doesn't merely tolerate boundaries—it demands them.

When you plan before you paint or draw, you have more freedom for your creative impulses as you work, less need to interrupt your work to make design decisions. Watercolorist John Pike used to say, "Plan like a turtle and paint like a rabbit." Organize the big things and the little things fall into place. When you design

first, you can put what is really important—*yourself*—into the picture. And, what is more important, when you know the rules, you can break them more creatively.

Students ask, "How do I know when a picture is finished?" Good question! Without a plan it's hard to tell. Design helps you get off to a good start and signals when you have finished.

In the classroom, many students are in such a hurry to start painting they miss the excitement that builds with creative planning. ***Artistic freedom functions best within a framework.*** Design enables you to make art spontaneously and intuitively. In his foreword

to *Form, Space, and Vision* by Graham Collier, Herbert Read wrote:

> *Spontaneity is not enough—or, to be more exact, spontaneity is not possible until there is an unconscious coordination of form, space, and vision.*

Planning and structuring your work won't stifle your creativity. What makes your design creative is how you use design to express your individuality. Each of us manipulates the elements and principles of design in a different way. It isn't the use of rules that stifles creativity—it's the lack of artistic vision. Design helps you to focus on your vision.

Beginning with the idea of jewel-like crystals embedded in rocks in a subterranean cavern, Keirns layered pieces of watercolor paper, then "discovered" the jewels as she painted into the layers with acrylics. The analogous palette with a hint of complementary contrast is unifying. The variations in shapes and sizes add interest. *Crystal Cave* by Lynn Keirns. Acrylic collage, 21" x 27". Collection of the Zanesville Art Center, Zanesville, Ohio.

Format

Design in drawing and painting is the arrangement of picture elements within a predetermined space to achieve a specific artistic objective. The most commonly used format for design is the rectangle. Begin your adventure into creative design by changing your format. Use a square, circle, oval; stretch your format until it is long and narrow. Turn your horizontal paper or canvas to the vertical. Expand it to a huge surface or reduce it to a miniature. Each change in the size or proportions of your support changes the way you present the subject.

Within the format you choose there are many options for placement of the subject and location of the center of interest. The entire space is at your disposal, not just the middle! To fit the subject in the format stretch it, squeeze it, bend it, float it, or shrink it. Push it beyond the edges of the support. Each approach changes the shapes and relationships of positive and negative elements.

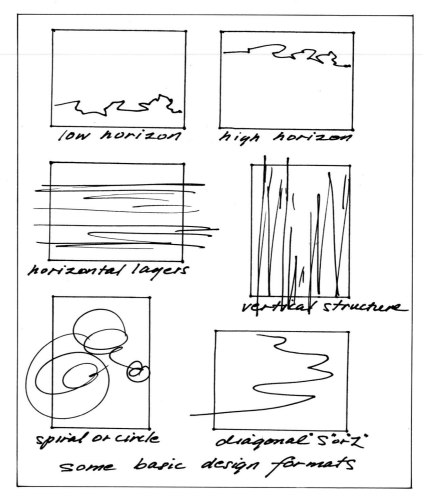

In addition to these basic design formats, you can probably come up with some variations of your own. Change the size or shape of the support, or relocate the center of interest within the format.

Activity

Draw three different formats on a page in your sketchbook/journal. Select an object such as a teapot, piggy bank, water pitcher, flower, or chicken and sketch some part of this shape within each format. Stretch it vertically within a tall, narrow format. Then let the subject run off the page of a square format. In the circle, mold the subject to fit the circular format. Play around with different sizes and shapes of format each time you plan a picture to discover unusual and interesting arrangements.

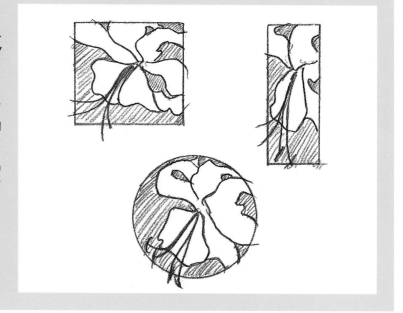

Different formats can spark your imagination.

Design Strategies

You probably wouldn't throw darts at a map to decide where you're going; you shouldn't design by accident, either. With intelligent and imaginative use of design you bring order from chaos, shaping nature into art. By manipulating design fundamentals, you make your pictures more creative without losing artistic integrity. They are meant to be used as guidelines, not inflexible rules.

Let's take a look at the elements and principles of design and how you can manipulate them to achieve different effects. Post these where you can see them at a glance:

Elements of Design	Principles of Design
Line	Unity
Shape	Harmony
Value	Contrast
Color	Rhythm
Movement	Repetition
Size	Gradation
Pattern	Balance
	Dominance

In realistic painting, the importance of shape is apparent when color and value are not gradated to create a photographic illusion of reality. Objects are easily recognized by their shapes, allowing the artist to be more creative with color and other elements of design and still remain faithful to the actual subject.

Untitled by Mel Meyer, S.M. Acrylic on canvas, 25" x 25".

Line

Judging by prehistoric drawings, line was the first of the elements of design to be used in two-dimensional art. Line describes contour or gesture, defines structure, and may be descriptive or decorative. Lines may be thick, thin, fast, slow, serene, agitated, jagged, lyrical, aggressive. Line brings energy to the design. A line drawn from one edge of a rectangle to another creates two shapes. The line acts as the boundary between the shapes: It divides, but also connects.

It's easy to overlook the creative possibilities of line, so always keep an eye out for how line quality can express your artistic concept.

Shape

You arrange shapes, whether realistic or abstract, to design your composition. The shape of an object is a positive shape. The background or the spaces between shapes are negative shapes. Plan both to enhance your design.

Make shapes visually interesting with varying dimensions and interlocking edges, like the pieces of a jigsaw puzzle. Plan the shapes first, then design your subject to fit the shapes.

Value

Value, the range between light and dark in the picture, has powerful expressive potential. A picture with strong value contrast has visual strength and makes a forceful statement. Use a high-key scheme (light values) to suggest an upbeat mood. To project a moody, introspective feeling, use a low-key value plan of darks and middle darks.

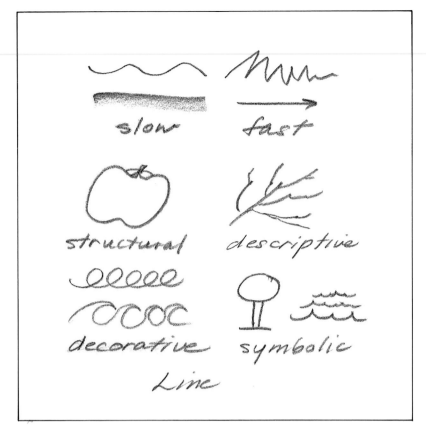

Line quality is an important design element that can make your paintings more expressive.

Several elements of design can be found in every picture, but one should dominate. This watercolor has texture, shape, and color, but it is value contrast that provides the drama. *Focus* by Nita Leland. Watercolor, 18" x 24". Private collection.

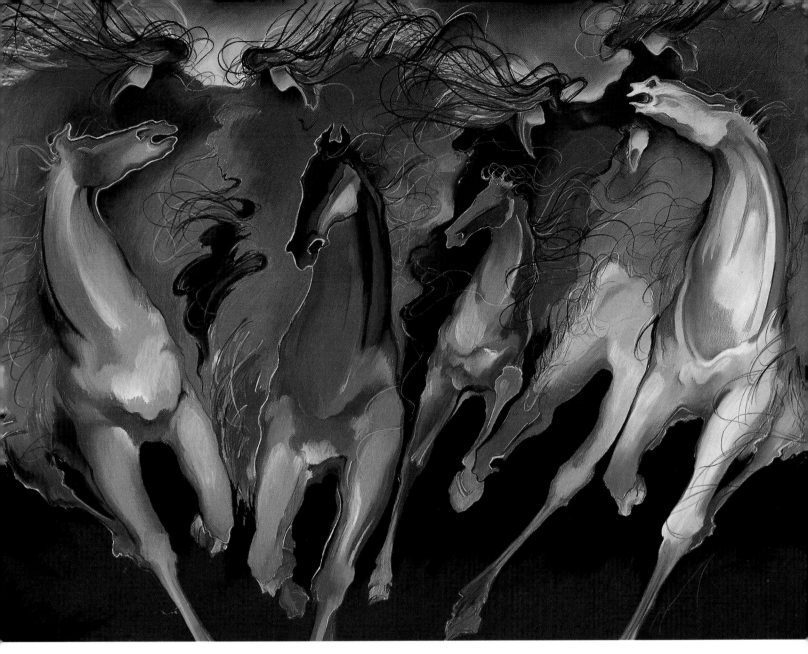

Color

Color is a highly expressive element of design. Learn the properties of color: *hue* (the name of the color, such as red or blue); *value* (the lightness or darkness of the hue); *intensity* (the purity or grayness of the hue); and *temperature* (the warmth or coolness of the hue). Use variations of the properties of color to change the mood. Compare a warm and a cool version of the same picture. Paint a picture in pure, unmixed hues. Do another variation modifying some of the colors to a lower intensity. Explore your colors to discover distinctive mixtures. Mix complements for exciting contrast and interesting hues. Use the colors you like best to show your "color personality." Start with a color idea and find a subject that suits the color. Do you feel "red" today? Paint red!

Color is even more expressive when you use creative color instead of painting things as they actually are. In this bold pastel, an analogous color scheme, including fully half of the color circle, is skillfully balanced. Notice how line reinforces the energetic movement. *Color Riders* by Bonny. Pastel, 50" x 72". © Bonny 1988. Courtesy of Houshang Youdim, Houshang's Gallery, Dallas, Texas.

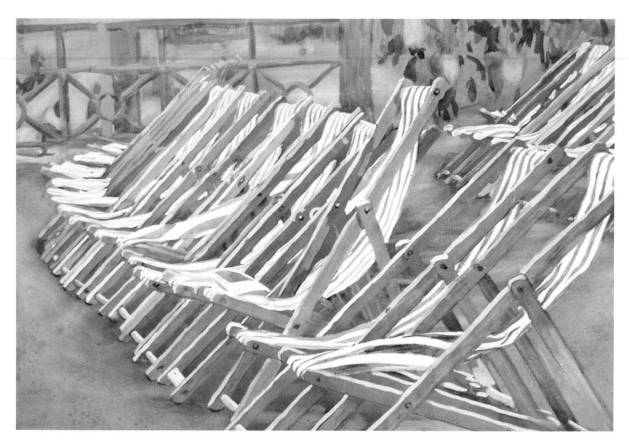

A row of empty beach chairs inspired this well-designed watercolor. The diagonal arrangement on the page suggests movement in a subject that might otherwise be relatively static. The background is muted, so it won't interfere with the strength of the pattern. *Brighton Airy* by Jan Upp. Watercolor, 21" x 28 ½". Collection of Peoples State Bank, St. Joseph, Michigan.

Barnum's tornado-like movement has everything in an uproar, but the locals seem firmly rooted to the ground and basically unconcerned. This contrast makes the picture lively and entertaining. *J. D.'s* by Robert Barnum. Watercolor, 16" x 21".

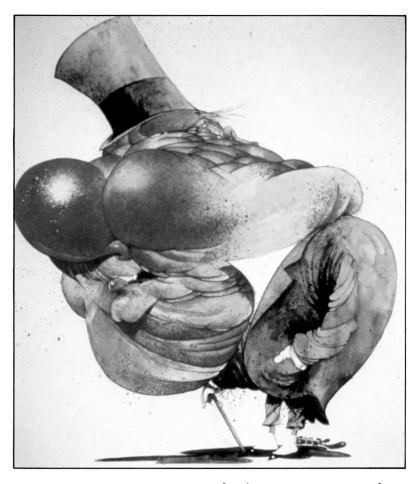

Distortion and exaggeration of proportions in a caricature quickly establish the personality of the subject. You might suspect, if you didn't already know it, that the gentleman depicted here was a bit of a curmudgeon and probably more than a little bit of a lush! *W. C. Fields* by Don Vanderbeek. Watercolor, 20" x 15".

Movement

Movement expresses life and energy in the picture, controls the speed of eye movement, and directs the viewer's eye to a focal point. There are three major types of movement. *Horizontal*, flat movement is restful and calm, such as a pastoral landscape, a quiet pond, or a reclining figure. The *vertical* suggests firmness and stability or growth, for example, a city skyline, a person standing at attention, or a forest of tall trees. Oblique, *diagonal* movement implies action, as in a crashing wave or a running figure. These same movements are used to create surface tension in abstract art. The dominant movement sets the pace for the dynamics of the picture.

Size

Scale denotes the size of people or objects in relation to their environment. Exaggerate scale by placing people in fantastic settings of huge, threatening size or by having them tower above a Lilliputian landscape. *Proportion* refers to size relationships of all parts of a whole: the hands in relation to the figure, the ears in relation to the head, the wheels in relation to the automobile. Correct proportions make a realistic picture believable. In abstract design, size relationships determine the visual impact of shapes and colors.

Pattern

Pattern uses lines, shapes, values, colors, and textures to enhance the surface and contribute to movement in the picture. The patterns in natural and manmade environments are a rich source of ideas: texture; growth patterns; and industrial, mechanical, building, and ornamental patterns. Use similar shapes and forms, for example, a dominant linear pattern or a predominance of dots and circles. Alternate patterned areas with quiet areas to give your viewer's eye a rest.

Activities

• Use 3" x 5" unruled index cards or trace rectangles in your sketchbook/journal. Work with pencil, pen, crayon, brush and watercolor, or a stick dipped in ink. Make one continuous line, crossing and recrossing, touching the borders on all four sides. Fill in the shapes that are trapped inside the crossing lines with color or value. Create a path of like-colored trapped shapes to help move the viewer's eye across the design. Continuity of line and color create a sense of unity in a design. Do two or three in black-and-white and color.

• Make a thumbnail value sketch of a still life, landscape, or portrait using strong value contrast. Reverse the value scheme in another sketch, changing darks to lights and vice versa.

• Make a high-key color sketch for an upbeat mood and a low-key sketch for a somber treatment of the same subject. Which approach to values seems most effective to you? Your choice of a value scheme determines the overall mood and visual impact of your picture.

• Build a design based on patterns from the environment. Make design sketches based on one or more of these patterns:

    a tree branch
    a stone wall
    a honeycomb
    cracks in the sidewalk
    stripes on a tiger
    a stack of dishes
    a slice of lemon

Superimpose decorative patterns on the natural pattern and create an eye path through the design by repeating colors, lines, shapes, or values.

Make trapped shapes and play with color or value to create a pattern or movement.

Reverse values to see what unusual effects you can create.

high key   low key

You can use an unexpected color key to make a forceful statement.

Unity

Unity is the organization of all the bits and pieces of a picture into a harmonious whole, your ultimate objective in the design process. When you are finished, there is a sense that nothing can be added or taken away. A unified design may be calm and contemplative or it may be aggressive and abrasive, but either way it must be consistent. The pieces are integrated into a coherent design. Unity in a work of art is intuitively felt even before you analyze how the artist has designed it.

Try to imagine this abstract without the bits of blue. Suppose the artist had used crimson instead of red-orange for the red accents or placed the shape in the lower left corner parallel to the edge. What do you think would happen to the design if you put a big flower in the middle of the circle? These changes would impair the balance and unity of the painting. *Key to the Universe* by Virginia Lee Williams. Sand, modeling paste, gel medium, acrylic paint, 18" x 34".

Activity

Examine the work of these two artists, who have distinctly different styles.

Does the work seem unified, complete?

Is the technique consistent?

Did the artist use design to reinforce the idea?

Can anything be added or taken away to improve the design?

These are subjective judgments. Keep an open mind! Write your ideas about unity in your sketchbook/journal. As you learn more about design, you'll become increasingly aware of specific ways artists use design to achieve unity.

Compare these two paintings to see how each artist unifies the design elements.

Inner Force by Pat Kelly. Collage: gold and silver spray-painted material and marbleized paper, 40" x 30".

Mountain Bell by Jăune Quick-to-See Smith. Acrylic and pastel on paper, 30" x 22". Courtesy of DEL Fine Art Galleries, Taos, New Mexico. Photography by F. A. Ambrose, Albuquerque.

Harmony

Harmony implies tranquility. A harmonious picture emphasizes similarities in relationships. Close values, colors adjacent on the color circle, and similarities of lines, shapes, and sizes are harmonious. Many artists paint harmonious pictures that are pleasing to look at.

To liven up a harmonious picture, introduce subtle variations: a slightly brighter color, a different line quality, an unusual format, an altered viewpoint, a tilted horizon line, an unexpected object, a bit of whimsy.

Contrast

Contrast is a dynamic factor, contributing excitement, attracting attention, and relieving monotony, like a sudden change of scenery on a long trip. Contrast creates tension between opposing elements: curved or straight, smooth or jagged, big or small, simple or ornate, bright or grayed, warm or cool. Opposites push and pull, energizing the picture surface and exciting the viewer's eye.

Introduce and control contrast to make a creative and stimulating picture. We usually think of using strong value contrast for immediate visual impact. You can also vitalize a low intensity color scheme with a sudden burst of pure color or energize flat shapes with a bold, aggressive line.

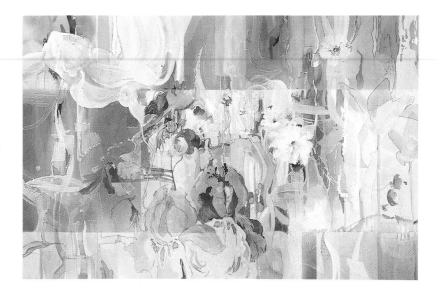

The high-key value plan keeps this painting harmonious. Gentle contrasts in complementary colors, a few middle-dark accents, subtle changes throughout in line, shape, and color make every area in the picture interesting without aggressive notes to spoil the mood. *Dream Series, Flora* by Joan Ashley Rothermel. Watermedia, 28" x 39".

Extreme contrast between the figure and the background underscores the idea of strong summer light. Super realism is most effective when it capitalizes on the sharp contrast characteristic of photographic film. *Summer Afternoon* by Gary Akers. Drybrush watercolor, 22" x 30".

Rhythm

Rhythm is defined as intervals at which related elements occur throughout a piece of art. Careful placement of accents pulls the viewer's eye across the picture at the will of the artist. The eye travels quickly when elements are closely spaced, more slowly across wider intervals. For example, in a landscape with trees, the eye will quickly scan a tight group of verticals, then pause at a clearing before moving on. A point of accent beyond the clearing resumes the rhythm. Your strongest accent creates a focal point or center of interest. Use accents to control the rhythm and keep the viewer's eye moving within the picture.

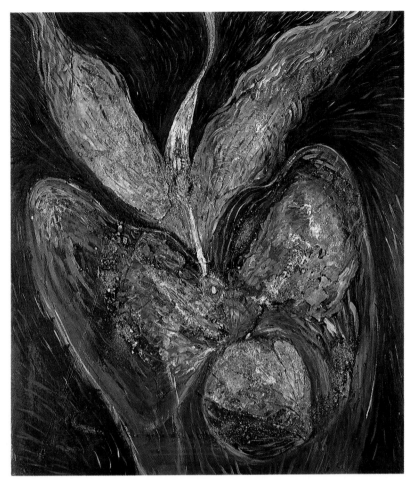

Follow the rhythmic curves of the shapes and the counterpoint of the short marks. Notice the different rhythm of the red strokes just below the center and the blues at the side with broken yellows intermixed with the blue. *Alchemy #5* by Beth Ames Swartz. 1987. Crystals, minerals, gold and silver leaf with mixed media on canvas, 72" x 60".

In this painting, musical rhythms became a picture. *Eternal Rhythm* by Nita Leland. Watercolor, 15" x 20".

Design **65**

Repetition

Repetition provides visual clues to help move the eye about the picture. The eye searches for related elements. Similarities in elements reinforce the viewer's recognition of symbols, strengthen the rhythm, encourage movement, and produce patterns. Direct the search so that each recurrence of a color, line, shape, or value leads the eye to your focal point. Introduce variations of repeated elements to prevent boredom. Pick up the vertical rhythms of a group of trees or a fence. Echo a cool background color in foreground shadows. Repeat a geometric shape in different sizes or colors.

Gradation

Gradual change implies movement. Slowly change a color from warm to cool, a value from light to dark, a line from thick to thin, a shape from small to large. Use gradation of size to suggest deep space. A sharp break in gradation interrupts movement through the picture, creating a rhythmic accent or establishing a focal point. You can unify contrasting elements by making a gradual transition between them or enhance areas that are plain and uninteresting by introducing subtle gradations of color or value.

Balance

Balance is the distribution of elements throughout the picture to produce equilibrium. In *symmetrical* balance, equal elements are equally divided on each side of a vertical axis. In *asymmetrical* balance, elements are unevenly divided, but are balanced according to visual weight. It is impossible to mea-

Notice the variations in the vertical forms—different sizes, shapes, and colors— and the punctuation marks of the little round eyes peering from the shadows. The diagonal at the top and the horizontals of the siding keep the vertical dominance from being too much of a good thing.
Back Porch Paradise by Don A. Snyder. Watercolor, 20 ¹⁄₁″ x 15 ¾″.

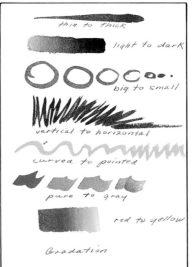

All kinds of gradation can be used to suggest movement or distance.

sure precisely the weight and tension of objects on a two-dimensional surface, so arrange and rearrange elements until they look "right." The more elements in the design, the trickier the balancing act.

Dominance

Dominance plays a central role in successful design, resolving conflict between elements and restoring unity to designs. Dominance is achieved through repetition, size, quantity, intensity, or movement.

Your dominant features are your star players, communicating your idea to the viewer. You decide which elements will govern. As you organize your composition, consider the potential for each element in supporting your concept. Some will be more effective for your purpose than others: these should dominate. When conflicts are resolved through dominance, the picture "works."

There is great stability in the vertical format and dominance of the tree forms. The elements are asymmetrically balanced, but so nearly equal that they contribute to a wonderful feeling of serenity. *Little Sugarcreek* by Bill Hurd. Chalk silkscreen, 34" x 26".

Most pictures that have a lot going on in them can be unified by a strong color dominance, as Sovek has done here. By contrasting the blue shadows with warm, light areas, he strongly suggests a bright, sunny day. Notice, too, how the diagonal direction of the foreground shadows leads the eye into the picture. *Blue Shadows* by Charles Sovek. Oil on canvas, 20" x 24". Private collection.

Design **67**

musical rhythm

beginning of an idea

Art, like music, has rhythms — experiment by using rhythm as the basis for a painting.

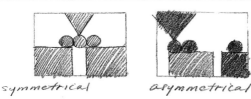

symmetrical   asymmetrical

You can balance shapes either symmetrically or asymmetrically.

line, pattern   shape, value   size, shape, value

Try changing the dominant element to achieve different effects.

● Turn on some music. On a large sheet of paper, "write" the rhythms of the music. Use flowing lines, geometric lines, hard lines, soft lines. Notice changes in rhythms and returns to a basic rhythm. Design pictures based on musical rhythms: waltz, ragtime, jazz, rock. Every picture you design should have an underlying rhythm, even if you paint or draw without music.

● Make a balanced symmetrical arrangement of a few simple organic or geometric shapes. Make an asymmetrical arrangement of the same or similar elements, balanced, yet not evenly divided. You can vary your design, adding more shapes and deliberately forcing imbalance for a more energetic design. When you plan a picture, establish simple visual balance first, then consider possible ways to make the picture more interesting by throwing it slightly off balance.

● Pick one element of design — line, value, shape, color, size, pattern, or movement — as the dominant factor in a sketch or painting and use it to express a definite mood. For example, use line or pattern to express the happy profusion of flowers in a country garden. Make another sketch changing the dominant element to create a dramatic change in the image and mood. You might combine shapes to unify the flower picture or enlarge the size of one or two flowers to fill the paper. Decide on one dominant element before you start each picture, but first explore several ideas.

Design Options

Don't be intimidated by rules. Matisse said, "Great art makes its own rules." Every rule is waiting to be broken! Just remember the two rules for breaking a rule: one is to fully understand it; the other is to know why you want to break it!

Your creativity is an expression of your uniqueness. Be yourself! Value your individuality. *Creativity is finding different ways of doing things.* Give your plan a twist or an element of surprise, even if it means breaking a rule. Here's how:

Look beyond what others see. Reveal the truth of the subject as you—and only you—perceive it. Search for your reality in the rhythms and patterns of nature. Discover the symbolism of shapes, lines, and colors. The symbols you select and the way you organize them convey your insights to your viewer.

Introduce elements not commonly associated with the subject or invent an unusual juxtaposition. Change a peaceful landscape by using hard edges, violent color, jarring contrasts. Interpret a floral bouquet by simplifying the profusion of blossoms and painting big geometric shapes. Be consistent throughout with your original idea. Continuity makes the picture work, giving it a sense of "rightness" from first stroke to last.

Each picture calls for a different solution. There are no sure-fire design formulas. The more planning you do at the beginning, the more likely you are to have a successful finish. The "happy accident" is a rare event.

This creative watercolor has everything going for it, beginning with an unusual treatment of a subject most people wouldn't think of: table napkins. The proportions of the dark and light background areas are just right, every diagrammatic line works to move the eye, and the marble creates the necessary focal point. *Right and Left Points to Center* by Janet Nicodemus. Watercolor, 22" x 30".

Creative Design

1. *Explore the subject in your sketchbook.* Does it call for a delicate touch or an explosion? Look for its gesture, the descriptive contours. Note important details.

2. *Identify your concept, theme, or idea.* Every composition should have a strong design emphasis. Every decision you make from here on out will depend on this.

3. *Determine design dominance to reinforce the concept.* Do you want:

- cool colors, restful horizontals?
- curving lines, hot colors?
- dynamic angles and obliques?
- large shapes or intricate patterns?
- sensitive colors or strong values?

4. *Choose a format that will enhance your expressive idea.* Use creative variations of design formats. Make distinctive choices in the layout of your picture, having your subject interact with the edges, forming interesting negative areas.

5. *Develop a design plan.* Make big shapes by combining several small shapes. Arrange lights and darks in an effective value pattern. Use your sketchbook to try different plans.

6. *Determine the focal point.* Place it a different distance from each edge. Plan rhythm, repetition, color, and pattern to direct the eye around the picture to your focal point. Arrange

Yes! Put your center of interest in the middle of the picture if you want to! Break rules, if necessary, to achieve the desired effect. *Z's a Crowd* by Marcia van Woert. Watercolor, 18" x 24".

your greatest contrasts of color and value there.

7. *Plan a distinctive color scheme.* Use the expressive quality of color and depend on dominance to support your concept.

8. *Decide on the medium and technique that will pull everything together.*

After watching a flock of Canadian geese take off and land, I wanted to express the surge of movement after takeoff. The cloud patterns in the background are part of the crossed diagonals formed by the heads pointing upward in one direction and the wings in the other. The dark value of the heads is dominant. *Rushing Wings* by Nita Leland. Watercolor, 22" x 30".

Activities

• Here are two basic design plans. Enlarge them on a piece of paper. Add line, color, value, or pattern to enhance each design. For example, repeat a pattern of value or color to suggest movement or introduce an energetic line to create tension. Add texture by rubbing your pencil or crayon over the paper with string, weeds, feathers, fabric, or other textured objects underneath it, or by printing paint or ink with leaves, sponges, cork, or fabric. Lay out a simple design of your own and develop it the same way. Think of every picture as a simple, basic design with surface design enhancement.

• Take control of an "accidental" design. Make your basic design plan on heavy paper. Dampen the paper slightly. Flow watercolor, acrylics, or ink onto the wet paper. Tilt the paper up, down, at an angle, following the directional movement of the basic design and establishing a color dominance. Add other elements if necessary to strengthen the design: line to emphasize the movement, value contrast to add visual impact and accents, shape definition to unify fragmented areas. Take advantage of the accidental effects of flowing paint as you resolve the design.

• Here are a few so-called "rules of design." You probably can add a few of your own.

—Keep the center of interest out of the middle of the picture.

—Keep the center of interest away from the edges of the picture.

—Always divide the picture in unequal parts.

—Always use uneven numbers of objects in a composition.

—Use warm colors in the foreground, cool ones in the background.

• Design a picture deliberately breaking one of these "rules of design." Decide why you are breaking it: to create a dramatic imbalance, to indicate absolute stability, to destroy the illusion of three dimensions, for example. Let your artistic intent in every picture determine whether the rule will prevail or you must break it to achieve your purpose.

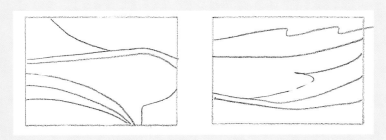

Enhance these basic design plans.

Henning takes a different direction with his geese, developing the image after the flow of ink on a dampened surface suggests the background. *Geese* by Fritz Henning. Inks, 10 ¼" x 11".

Planning the arrangement of objects in a still life is one of the design tasks of the realistic artist. One way to assure unity in the picture is to use related objects, as Weber does here. The consistent quality of light is also effective.
Mason Mallards by Michael J. Weber, A.W.S. Transparent watercolor, 14" x 20".

Chapter 4

Realism: Taking the Scenic Route

"The faculty of creating is never given to us all by itself. It always goes hand in hand with the gift of observation. And the true creator may be recognized by his ability to find about him, in the commonest and humblest thing, items worthy of note."

Igor Stravinsky, The Poetics of Music

Realistic art is a celebration of life! From the grandeur of the landscape to the humble tools in your kitchen cabinets, everything is subject material. Realism is the representation of objects in the physical world, the external things that are a large part of your inner experience. Their pictorial images are clearly recognized by the viewer, although they may be stylized in a number of ways.

Realistic painting is every bit as creative as making an abstract. Realism is viewed by many as the opposite of abstraction, but in actuality, all good realistic painting has sound abstract structural design. You use the design elements to communicate with your viewer, making your realistic picture more than a record of what the subject looks like.

Instead of moving in opposite directions, the paths of realism and abstraction run parallel. Artists move between them freely. Our approaches differ because we have different ideas of what is fun or challenging to do. Our ideas on that might change at any time. In *Search for the Real*, abstract expressionist Hans Hofmann wrote:

It makes no difference whether (a) work is naturalistic or abstract; every visual expression follows the same fundamental laws.

Artist Georgia O'Keeffe felt this way about the dispute over realism versus abstraction:

It is surprising to me to see how many people separate the objective from the abstract. Objective painting is not good painting unless it is good in the abstract sense. A hill or a tree cannot make a good painting just because it is a hill or a tree. It is lines and colors put together so that they say something.

Realistic painting can be very personal. From the moment you select the subject to the instant you sign the finished piece, whatever you paint or draw reflects your subjective interpretation. Your art reveals your personal relationships with family, friends, and neighborhood; your cultural heritage and religion; your education and training. Twenty artists painting the same subject at the same time and place will come up with twenty different renderings. The subject is transformed as it filters through unconscious thought processes to reflect past experiences and inner convictions.

There is a difference between *image* and *essence* in realistic art. One artist goes to the mountain carrying painting gear, sketches it, sets up the easel, and paints a realistic illusion of the mountain—its image. Another artist sits in contemplation of the mountain

By placing realistic figures on the flat planes of an abstract background suggesting a house and yard, Barnes lends a timeless, bigger-than-life quality to an ordinary setting. Although very much alive, the figures seem frozen in suspended motion against the flat background. *Backyard* by Curtis Barnes. Oil on cotton canvas, 36 ½" x 48 ½".

Mulhollen's watercolor describes a common scene in a dramatic light. The skillful handling of medium and design underscores the artist's perception of the subject. Another artist might do it differently, but it would be hard to do it more beautifully. *Winter Feed* by Jack Mulhollen. Watercolor, 19" x 29". Collection of the artist.

for a while, turns his back to it and paints *mountain* — its essence. The goal for most realists is to successfully combine image and essence.

There's nothing totally new in art. Your choice of subject may be unusual or quite ordinary, but what you do with it makes it special. You have something of your own to say about that subject. Instead of reporting unimportant details, reveal your perception of the subject through your selection and arrangement of colors, lines, shapes, and other design elements. Your art is creative because of your individuality. Art is about communication, insights, feelings, not just a recital of facts.

When you ask yourself, "What shall I paint or draw?" the only good answer is "anything and everything"! I've seen wonderful drawings of mop buckets and terrific paintings of table napkins. Open your eyes and consider the creative possibilities of everything you see: cityscape, farmscape, seascape, woodland, desert, rocks, flowers, trees, wildlife, mountains, reflections, dolls, backyard, junkyard, sunlight, moonlight, lamplight . . . keep going!

Start with familiar, picturesque, traditional subjects and look for novel ways to use them. But don't stop there. Widen your search beyond the obvious. Do some brainstorming: write down things you love, things you hate. List objects, people, places, experiences. Look for your themes and symbols. Sketch out possible design treatments. Keep the list going and refer to it when you're stuck for subject matter.

Once you have found your realistic subject, you have two major objectives: to create an abstract design incorporating the subject, and to present the subject in a distinctive, personal way.

Activities

● Analyzing the work of other artists makes you more aware of ways you can strengthen abstract design in your own realistic pictures. Place tracing paper over pictures in this book to screen out detail so you can look for the big shapes and values and linear movements. These are the abstract design elements that unify the picture. Analyze the value pattern for contrast and value key, the color design for expression. Pick out the dominant design element that establishes unity. You can also squint at a picture to see the overall design or view slides out-of-focus. Shapes, values and color relationships become more apparent when detail is blurred.

● Pick a subject from the list in your sketchbook, for example, trees. Ask yourself what design factors are naturally present and emphasize these in a sketch. In the example, the vertical direction, lines and textures of foliage and bark, branching growth pattern, and linear calligraphy of branches would qualify. Look for a design approach that you may have previously overlooked: Had you noticed the way the branches radiated from the trunk as seen from below? That the veins on the leaves branch out just like the branches from the tree? Introduce a design element that isn't there: a decorative pattern on the leaves or trunk or a fantastic color scheme.

How are the apples in Weber's painting related to the antique objects? That depends on the viewer's associations. I suspect there might be maple syrup in the jug, pickles in the crock, and applesauce cooking on the stove. What do you think?
Stoneware with Apples by Michael J. Weber. Watercolor, 18" x 24".

You and Your Subject

How do you determine what will be a good subject for a picture?

- Should you search for something exotic and unique?
- What if you prefer a simple subject?
- Why do you choose a particular subject?
- Why does it interest you?
- What do you see in this subject that another person might not see?
- How would you communicate this in a picture?

You don't really choose a subject. *The subject chooses you.* It attracts your attention and insists, "Do me!" Even if the subject isn't new, your interpretation of it will be unique. Make your experience of the subject real for others. Get excited about it. Get your viewer involved.

The foundation of design will help you to turn your most sincerely felt emotions into art. My Jewish friend Rebecca is deeply religious. Much of her work includes symbolism from her religion. It is not sentimental representation. Although there are realistic objects in her pictures, the pictures aren't about "things." Rebecca makes pictures about what these things mean to her. This subtle reference commands the viewer's attention and respect.

When you paint or draw, you are making visible something that cannot be expressed in words. This includes not only the appearance of the subject, but also your ideas about it and the intensity of your emotional involvement with it.

In fact, you are the subject. In his *Journal* Eugène Delacroix wrote,

Everything is a subject; the subject is yourself. It is within yourself that you must look and not around you. . . . The greatest happiness (is) to reveal it to others, to study oneself, to paint oneself continually in (one's) work.

Only the germ of an idea is needed to start the creative process. First, you see a thing. Your brain tells you what you know about it, shaping your perception. Start out with a simple subject — for example, an apple. Take note of the object's physical appearance, color, texture, and smell: crimson red with areas of golden yellow, speckled, smooth and roundish, bumpy on the end, brown stem, worm hole on one side, spicy smell.

Search your mind for past associations: the smell of fresh apple pies baking or applesauce cooking — with cinnamon, of course. Picking apples from the twisted trees in an old orchard and canning applesauce. A tummy ache from eating green apples. Feeding an apple to a gentle pony. Planting an apple tree. Find yourself in your subject; stop to think about it.

Make contour drawings from several angles. Slice the apple and draw the cross section, too. Take a bite and "draw" the taste: crisp and chewy, a little bit tart — yummm!

Why, in the middle of the surging crowds of the city, does Hollerbach record this particular group of people? Even if the scene is a composite of many he has observed, what caused him to put these people in this place at this time — in just this way? It was because the subject grabbed him and he felt compelled to shape it into a work of art. *Street Scene in Upper Manhattan* by Serge Hollerbach. Acrylic on board, 40″ x 40″.

Mendoza's sensitive still life shows how an artist invents a personal interpretation of ordinary objects using elements of design and the artist's own "touch" with the medium. *A Touch of Porcelain* by John L. Mendoza. Watercolor and gouache, 30" x 22".

If It Feels Good, Paint It

I'm convinced there is no such thing as a "bad" subject. Your attention to a subject makes it important. The subject itself doesn't communicate with the viewer; you do. It doesn't even matter whether or not your viewer agrees with you. What matters is that he or she reacts.

Most of us lean toward visually pleasing subject matter for our pictures. Surface prettiness soon loses its charm. Take command and use the power of design to create a unique expression of how you see the subject. Create an unusual color scheme; use dramatic value contrast; emphasize texture, pattern, or line.

Flowers, fishing shacks, lighthouses, and barns—some call these clichés. But if you grew up on the desert, a fishing shack is a novelty. In a rain forest, a lighthouse isn't commonplace. So follow your intuition in selecting a subject. If something intrigues you, it is worthy of exploration. Look for its creative possibilities.

No matter how often a subject has been done, when you integrate your concept of it with your special touch with a medium, the result is a new reality, something that never existed before. That's creativity!

Never mind if the subject has been done by others. Do something unusual with the obvious. You have your own way of doing things. Your approach to a subject may change many times, making it a rich source of imagery over and over again.

You can paint or draw whatever you like without apology. As author/painter Henry Miller said, "Paint as you like and die happy!"

For years Don quit painting because he had a watercolor teacher who described wildlife artists as "fin and feathers freaks." Eventually he realized he was cheating himself by deferring to another's opinion of what would make suitable subject matter for him. Today he enjoys success painting his birds and beasts, because others take as much pleasure in looking at them as he does in painting them!

Explore any subject when you feel you have something to say about it. Another artist may seem more successful at selecting unusual subject matter, but those subjects may not be down your alley. You paint best what you know best. Feel free to be creative with the familiar.

My students favor landscapes because that is what I do. With encouragement and instruction I urge them to try other subjects. Marianne painted drab little landscapes until the lesson on portraits. Faces turned everything around for her. Marianne is a "people person," and has something to say when she paints them.

Picturesque is in the eye of the beholder. Each viewer comes to your picture with a different set of perceptions.

Using a pointillist technique not often seen today, Cain organizes patterns and objects her own way. From her selection of objects to her decision to reflect the fruit in a mirror, the artist refines the general idea of still life to the particular image in her picture. *Still Life with Cherries* by Karen Cain. Gouache, 18" x 24".

Warren couldn't understand why I enjoyed painting watercolors of barns. For me, a barn revived memories of rowdy family reunions with my grandmother's kin. Barns reminded him of rats! You can't please everyone, but you can connect with those who feel as you do.

Subject matter can't be selected by formula. Ken kept a tight inventory control over the work he exhibited at outdoor art fairs: fifteen barns, six tropical scenes, ten seascapes, eight florals. When he sold one from any category, he went home and painted another for the next show. He repeated himself so much that buyers eventually tired of his work. And so, by the way, did he!

An oil painting of slides of oil paintings—what a creative idea! See how many subjects you can find in the next ten minutes that you would not ordinarily think of as worthwhile for a realistic painting. Consider the possibilities! *Slidescape* by Peggy McCarty. 1988. Oil, 29 ½" x 45".

Activities

• You can make ordinary subject matter more interesting with an unusual design treatment. Arrange five or more objects for a still life. Change your position two or three times as you draw the objects—standing, sitting, moving to one side or behind the setup. Draw the objects as you see them from the different angles, but distort or exaggerate if necessary to strengthen the design on the page. Reinforce continuity of line and dynamic movement instead of reporting what you see from a single point of view.

• Pick any subject from your list. Invoke a sense of mystery. Use soft edges and close values. Eliminate detail. Select unusual colors rather than local colors. Or reveal a powerful feeling about the subject with violent color and agitated gestural lines. There is nearly always a more interesting way to handle a subject than to present it the way you find it.

Change eye levels to help you find unusual angles on your subject.

Sources of Imagery

Where are you going to find source material for your realistic artwork? Every artist has difficulty with this question now and then. In the classroom students often copy the work of other artists. Much better sources are your own photographs and working from life. Also, use your imagination and your sense of humor to create realistic images.

Copying the work of other artists is sometimes done to practice skills and techniques, but there are many pitfalls to copying. It is impossible to capture the emotion expressed by the artist in the original. A copyist may be copying mistakes and second-rate methods without realizing it. Furthermore, copying prevents you from learning to organize a picture on your own.

The creative experience is missing when you copy. Eva was enrolled in a class that cop-ied pictures every week. This was boring, so she quit painting. Later, working in my class with original source material rekindled her enthusiasm.

Some people become dependent on copying. Rob was a gifted copyist but unable to create original art. The simplest solutions evaded him, and he struggled with basic techniques. Only by moving beyond copying could he become a genuinely creative artist.

Students who copy should clearly understand that they must not sign the work and may not sell or exhibit it except in a student show, and then only if the proper attribution is made to the original artist.

Copying is not as satisfying as doing your own work, even if the copied picture looks more "professional." Take pride in doing your own work. Strengthen your creative muscle along with your skills.

Your photographs are fine source material for your artwork. The camera enables you to develop a subject without having it right before your eyes. Your personal involvement with the scene will be revealed in your picture, even when details are not visible in the photo. You have a reason for taking the photo. Later, you paint it for the same reason.

Lydia began a watercolor in class based on her photo of a high, rounded hill rising out of

After you finish chuckling over the pun in Brower's super-realistic picture, try to imagine how he arrived at the final statement. First, he discovered the play on words, then he visualized the arrangement of the objects that would communicate this to the viewer. And finally, as an added note of humor, he decided he'd better let us know he didn't make a mistake. The artist's wit is as much the subject of the picture as the pun. *Pardon My French* by Jim Brower. Transparent watercolor, 14" x 23".

Light is fleeting and difficult to capture on location. But if you work from slides or photographs, you have to deal with the fact that the photo rarely duplicates that special quality you were attracted to in the first place. Instead of copying the photograph literally, re-create what is stored in your memory. As in this painting, the result is a blend of what you saw and what you felt. *River Patterns* by Robert Frank. Pastel, 22" x 29".

a lake, taken from a boat. It was a "nothing" photo, but I tried not to dampen her obvious enthusiasm. Imagine my surprise later when I looked at her painting over her shoulder and saw dozens of quaint, Irish cottages on the hill! "They were on the other side of the hill," she told me, "but by the time I got my camera ready, they were out of sight." But not out of Lydia's mind!

Some artists prefer photographs, others work from slides. Either way, be selective and imaginative rather than literal, in your use of the material. Look for unusual effects to make a more creative picture:

- Some types of camera lenses cause distortion. Emphasize this.
- The eye level may be tilted because the photographer tilted the camera. Try using this in your picture.
- Ambiguous light sources may affect shadows and forms strangely. Take advantage of these peculiarities if they make a more expressive picture.
- If the contrast is weak, make up a single, dramatic light source.

The camera makes no judgments, so you must. Even a well-composed photograph needs editing to become a forceful painting or drawing.

Activities

A viewfinder can help you find an interesting composition within a larger design or photograph.

- Take an experimental photo field trip, deliberately distorting every picture you shoot, for example:
  —Tilt the camera at a 45 degree angle.
  —Move the camera horizontally or vertically as you press the release button.
  —Shoot a closeup too close for the range of the camera.
  —Place the camera on top of your head and shoot straight up.
  —Stand in one place and turn in a circle, shooting four photos as you turn.
  —Shoot a couple of pictures inside without a flash, toward a window.
  —If you have them, use fisheye, telephoto, or zoom lenses for special effects.
  Use one of these photographs as the source for a painting or drawing.
- Photographs are rarely perfect compositions. Look for compositions within a photo by moving a small viewfinder or an empty slide mount over the photo. You may discover several good designs in one picture. Make thumbnail sketches of the compositions you find. Use one of these small sketches for a picture without referring to the photo. This approach gives you lots of leeway in design planning and helps you to become less dependent on the source photo as you develop your picture.

Getting Close to Nature

On-the-spot painting and drawing supplies you with a wealth of realistic subject matter. Working from life includes direct observation of a subject out-of-doors or inside with a still life; the clothed figure in its natural environment or the nude model in the studio.

Nature supplies a multitude of subjects, but nature itself is not art. You pick and choose, simplify and rearrange, until you have transformed the subject from a literal image into visual expression. Your viewer should sense what the picture is about without being distracted by a recitation of irrelevant facts.

Nature is rich in subject matter and generous with detail. An artist can easily become confused. Design helps you focus on essentials and turn nature into art without merely depicting what things look like.

Choose a design element that is appropriate to what you want to express and focus on that in your picture. In the next picture pick a different element and take off in another direction.

When you work directly from nature, observe carefully. If you are working with the illusion of reality, be correct. Viewers are easily sidetracked by inaccuracies. Suggest deep space by placing lighter values and cooler colors in the distance, by overlapping objects and converging parallel lines, or by making distant objects smaller.

Sense your personal reaction to the special qualities of the subject. What lies beneath the surface? Make up a story about it — about the happy family that lived in the old historic house a hundred years ago, or the tragic fate of the fisherman who sailed out from the rocky coast, or the paths by which the different objects in your still life came together to become your subject.

Select the aspects of the subject that will best express its inner nature or your ideas about it. You can take the subject out

The iris is one of the most beautiful spring flowers, partly because of its majestic vertical growth pattern. Barr has noticed two blossoms that, crowded out of the bunch, crept along the ground to find the sun and explode into bloom like orchids in the wild. You'll find myriads of such wonderful surprises in nature if you look for them. *Iris Reaching Out* by Ave Cassell Barr. Watercolor, 17 ¼" x 32".

of context if necessary to make your statement: a wildflower blooming on Times Square or an igloo in the desert.

Through the process of elimination, condense the subject to a manageable number of components. Keep it simple. Reduce the number of objects, simplify the shapes, eliminate detail. Organize these separate parts using the elements and principles of design to create a coherent work of art from the raw materials of nature.

You are bombarded by subject matter for realistic art! It takes creativity to find worthwhile subject matter in a humble object. I assigned a class the task of painting a "found" still life at home. Carla brought in a wonderful picture of her ironing board, iron, shirts on hangers, and a pile of laundry in the basket. Now *that's* an unlikely subject! But who wouldn't rather paint than iron?

Understanding perspective helps you to paint scenes like this. Notice how the cool buildings at center recede into the background behind the warmer buildings. The darker values at left stay forward as lighter values suggest distance. *Soho* by Charles Sovek. Oil on canvas. 24" x 18". Private collection.

Activities
• Concentrate on a single fresh flower. What do you want to express when you paint or draw this flower?

The richness of its color? Select a bold color scheme.

Its delicacy and fragility? Choose a high-key pastel scheme or an understated line.

The intricate tracing of its lacy petals? Emphasize line and pattern.

Think of other qualities you might express about this flower and the design elements that you could use to express them. Make a painting or drawing from one of your designs.

• Open a closet, look in your garage or a corner of the yard, visit a junkyard. You'll need to resolve the design. Focus on five to seven objects and develop a picture. Unify your picture by finding or creating common elements: a similarity of shapes, sizes, colors, lines. Use distortion if necessary. Make a drawing or painting.

A master of character portraiture, Hacker's interest in people is revealed in a straightforward manner. In this richly detailed face the eyes are the riveting focal point. Color helps him to express warm feelings about his friend. *Hal Scroggy* by Homer O. Hacker, A.W.S. Watercolor, 14" x 21".

Powers communicates a very different sentiment here—dejection. The cool blues and violets, along with the sketchy linear treatment, support that concept. I sense that the format makes its contribution, too, locking the subject into a rigid square from which there seems no escape. *Down and Out* by Alex Powers. Watercolor and charcoal, 23" x 23". Private collection, Lexington, Kentucky.

No matter how realistic you want your painting to be, you must mold it into a work of art. Brommer's collage process calls for several stages of development, gradually changing the real scene to make a better picture. No doubt the subject is easily recognized by those familiar with it, but there is a lot of Brommer in the picture, too. *Two Lights, Maine* by Gerald F. Brommer. Watercolor and collage, 22" x 30".

Barrish's stylized approach to a similar subject is his unique way of saying something about it. Remember, there is no "right" way. Every artist has a different way. *York Harbor, Maine* by A. Joseph Barrish, S.M. Markers, 12" x 9".

Painting the Realistic Subject

You've selected your subject. Now what? Even the ideal subject must be shaped and trimmed to fit the idea you want to express. The visual aspect alone isn't enough. A camera can record that. What do you want to say? What is the best way to say it?

These are two very important questions. Your answers set the direction and tone for your creative effort. Every aspect of your art comes into play: choice of medium, type of support, your individual technique, selection of design principles. You need a strategy to help you get on the road.

Make a list of descriptive words that characterize the subject—its physical appearance and essential qualities that make it unique or of interest to you. These might be intangible qualities like a mood or emotion. They might be physical attributes describing texture (smooth, rough, lacy), shape (crooked, sensuous, jagged), color (exotic, brilliant, delicate), or contrasts (light/dark, smooth/rough, big/small).

Get as many ideas as possible. ***Then narrow these down to one clear meaning.*** This is your concept. Concentrate on this. Artist Charles Hawthorne said:

> *Painting is just like making an after-dinner speech. If you want to be remembered, say one thing and stop.*

Turn to page 70 and review the steps in creative design. Follow the same procedure for organizing your realistic subject.

Even without the title, it's pretty clear this painting is about sun and shadow. All other considerations are secondary to the strong value patterns created by the light: no features in the figure or flowers, no textured leaves on the trees. The visual strength of a simple statement is usually more effective than a litany of detail. *Afternoon Sun: Nelson, New Zealand* by Peggy McCarty. 1988. Oil, 18" x 31".

Activity

Select a subject from one of your photos or sketches. Work out a series of three design plans for the subject. Use the "zoom lens" approach:

—Start with a middle-range view of the subject in a background.

—Zoom in until the subject fills the frame and the background is reduced to negative shapes around the edges of the frame.

—Zoom in again for a close-up of some part of the subject.

Change the color, the center of interest, the format, the medium, the value plan.

Add linear design, textural interest, decoration, imaginary elements.

Emphasize a particular quality of light or a seasonal ambience.

Contrast light and dark for dramatic effect; change to misty, soft shapes in high-key or values; switch from glowing warm autumn color to icy cold winter blues in the next picture.

Don't always paint the first design you come up with. Plan several approaches to push yourself beyond the obvious.

This painting typifies good abstract art. The design qualities of shape, color, and texture are paramount without the need to create a realistic image.
Riddles of the Earth by Virginia Lee Williams. Gesso, tissue paper, gauze, acrylic paint, 20" x 24".

Chapter 5

Abstraction: Off the Beaten Path

"Abstract Art has come into being as a necessary expression of the feelings and thoughts of our age; it has added new dimensions to creative painting; it is part of the constant change and vital searching that energizes every true art."

Leonard Brooks, Painting and Understanding Abstract Art

An artist with an open mind will discover that realism and abstraction have a great deal in common. The truth is, abstract and realistic art are simply two aspects of the same thing: using the elements and principles of design to shape an artwork. If you can do one, you can do the other. What's more, *experimenting with abstraction can help you tap into whole new aspects of your own creativity.*

The primary difference is that realism represents a clear image of what you see in the physical world, while abstraction is the process of refining and reorganizing a realistic image or a mental concept to reveal the "essence"—the essential nature—of a subject, without regard for its physical appearance. Art that is pure design without apparent reference to a subject is called nonobjective, nonfigurative, or nonrepresentational.

Not all artists begin as realists, but many do. Quite a few are able to move back and forth successfully between realism and abstraction. It's all the same thing: expression in art. Follow this new direction and I predict one of two things will happen: your realistic design will carry greater authority or you will become a confirmed abstract artist!

Leonard Brooks in *Painting and Understanding Abstract Art* says,

Today, in most civilized circles, there is no need to break swords over the question of Abstract versus Realism because the value and sincerity of much of the Abstract movement has proven itself to be the extension of a legitimate and valid language of the painter.

One way to create abstractions is to use design to alter a literal image. With every change, the image moves farther from the illusion of reality. The more changed the image, the more abstract the art. Eventually, it may become pure abstraction, showing little or no connection with the original subject. Intelligent use of design makes it work.

Georgia O'Keeffe said,

Sometimes I start in a very realistic fashion, and as I go on from one painting onto another of the same kind, it becomes simplified till it can be nothing but abstraction. . . .

Whichever path you follow, learn to understand and appreciate all art. As you look at and analyze art in galleries, museums, books, and magazines, you expand your potential for growth and change in your own work. If you're a realist, try abstraction. You'll like it! If you're a good abstractionist, emphasize design and you'll be even better.

This colorful silkscreen has retained the idea of a floral bouquet without representing the image of a flower. A few more steps and the design might be abstracted into bands of color bearing no resemblance to the original subject. *Bridget's Bouquet* by Bobbi Ameen. Serigraph, 21″ x 14″.

Activity

Seeing abstract design gets easier with practice. Move a 35mm slide mount or 1″ x 1¼″ frame over the realistic art in the previous chapter. Find small abstract designs to record in your sketchbook/journal. Note what you like about each one: values, colors, arrangement of shapes, line quality, or directional emphasis. You might also devise designs of your own, arranging geometric shapes or ''scribble'' designs in your sketchbook. Use these sketches as beginnings for some of the exercises in abstraction in this chapter.

Train your eye to look for abstract designs.

Landmarks of Abstraction

Since you're not restricted to a literal image when you make abstract art, the sky's the limit—almost! Abstraction isn't just a series of happy accidents, however. Remember: Your creativity flourishes when you set limits to keep things under control. Find out what keeps the wheels of abstraction turning. Abstract picture-making is conducive to creative thinking. Both the real world and your inner world provide good starting points.

Extracting an essence is the primary object of abstraction. The *American Heritage Dictionary* defines abstraction as "the act or process of separating the inherent qualities or properties of something from the actual physical object or concept to which they belong." This means eliminating the literal and emphasizing the intangible. In short, redesigning nature to reflect your personal responses to it.

Formal relationships take the principal role in organizing an abstract picture. Some abstract pictures depend almost entirely on the formal aspects of design. Without relying on the subject itself to suggest meaning, they use design to express an idea. Soon we'll look at ways to use the basic design factors in abstract pictures.

A third factor to consider in abstraction is the importance of the *two-dimensional pictorial space*. The picture on your flat paper or canvas can look flat when you give up the illusion of three dimensions that is characteristic of realism. You are affirming that nothing in the picture is "real," freeing yourself of the obligation to make it look real.

Every painting, whether abstract or realistic, has to start somewhere. Where does one like this originate? From several possible beginnings: the selection of certain materials or size, a particular color combination or maybe an "accidental" beginning with flowing paint. The rest depends on the artist's concept or idea, which may start the action or may come into play as the materials interact. *Ancient Rumors #5* by Katherine Chang Liu. Mixed media on paper: watercolor, gouache, collage, 30" x 40". Courtesy of Louis Newman Galleries, Los Angeles.

In abstract design, you can:

1. Reverse values, change shapes, alter colors to suppress the illusion of deep space.
- Place warm colors and dark values in the background.
- Enlarge distant shapes to bring them closer.
- Eliminate recession and gradation into space.

2. Establish a visually flat picture space.
- Discard converging lines or converge lines in the foreground instead of the background.
- Use several different eye levels in the same picture, along with tilting planes.

3. Suggest ambiguous space with floating objects, advancing and receding shapes.

4. Eliminate background and foreground. Connect objects to the edges of the paper, making the support their environment.

Even without reference to real objects there is an illusion of shallow space in this beautifully designed abstract. Warm colors and lighter values advance, while cool hues and darks recede. *Secret Chamber II* by Carole Myers, N.W.S. Acrylic/collage on paper, 29" x 21".

Activities

- Pick a design from the small sketches you made in the previous activity. Assign one or more descriptive words to it — something you would like to express using this design. Choose colors, lines, values, and patterns that support the idea or feeling you want to convey. You control the expression in the design by the elements you choose. Make a color sketch or painting. Remember: One element must dominate.

- Your sketchbook/journal should have lists of images for realistic pictures. Add action words, descriptive words, emotional words to the lists: absurd, angry, apathetic, bold, beautiful, brittle, and so on. Select at random an image word and descriptive word as a point of departure for an inventive abstraction: absurd/garden; angry/forest; brittle/chair. Abstract the image to reflect the description — a new "essence" for the subject. As you develop your picture, select design elements that reflect this essence. Your end result will not be a literal image of a garden, for example, but rather a strange abstraction.

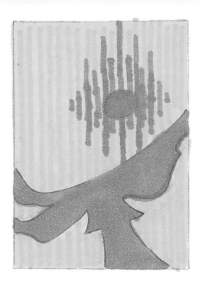

Use the elements of design to convey an idea or emotion in your abstract work.

Three Steps to Abstract Art

There are three major steps in making abstract art just as in realistic art: *exploration, development,* and *execution.* The biggest difference is in the exploratory phase. The realistic artist searches for ways to represent the visual appearance of the subject, while the abstract artist is looking for the means to *overcome* physical appearance and describe a hidden essence. Abstraction isn't difficult; it's just different.

Exploration

Abstract picture-making begins with the selection of a subject, theme, or motif. Anything can be abstracted. Why do you pick a certain subject or idea for your abstraction? For any reason—or no reason. Because it's there. Abstraction and non-objective pictures run the gamut from deeply personal expression to formal analysis of design with many levels in-between. Do you like birds? Their songs? Their coloration? Their mannerisms? Their freedom to soar above the earth?

The power of large birds in flight? Can you tell about it without making a picture of a bird? That's abstraction!

Verbalizing helps to capture the essence, especially if you want to abstract a feeling or experience instead of an object. List words that describe the feeling or synonyms for it: for example, serenity is cool, drifting, quiet, peaceful. Invent metaphors for it: for example, serenity is the calm sea of life; anger is a festering wound.

Drawing clarifies the essence for you. Decide what particular quality interests you in the subject or theme. Make a page of pencil marks with your eyes closed, "drawing" words that describe the subject: horizontals, verticals, angles, curves, scratches, blobs. Draw lines and shapes that symbolize feelings. Concentrate on what you want to emphasize in your abstraction. Say one thing. Reduce your theme to a manageable expressive concept.

Development

The developmental phase takes the adventure a step fur-

ther: the discovery of new ways of saying things, translating the drawn or the verbal image into the language of abstraction. Simplify! Stylize! Ask yourself questions:

- Can I reduce this, enlarge it, distort it, accent it?
- What materials would work best with my interpretation?
- What techniques would enhance it?
- Which should dominate: color or line? value or shape? size? movement? pattern? repetition, gradation, conflict, harmony?

Execution

By this time you are ready to roll. You've played with ideas and words, gaining insight into what you want to say about the subject and some ways to accomplish this. Play with your materials, sketch different designs, be flexible and ready for change. Each time one thing changes, everything changes. Look for the changes and be ready to move off in new directions.

Stage 1. Ed Betts begins with a "largely unconscious improvisation . . . (as) a way of getting things going pictorially."

Stage 2. Betts begins to develop the subject by painting shapes of rocks and surf into the colorful, undefined masses.

"The end result," says Betts, "is a consciously controlled arrangement of colors, shapes, and textures that refer to nature but do not imitate or copy it." *Northcoast* by Edward Betts. Acrylic, 40" x 50". Private collection. Photograph courtesy of Midtown Galleries, Inc., New York City.

Directions in Abstraction

Realism to Abstraction

Working from a realistic image toward abstraction is a reduction process. The subject is reduced to simple shapes and lines. You eliminate superfluous detail and accent only the essentials. The painting or drawing retains the image, but is stylized to emphasize the qualities you want to express. Symbolic lines and colors refer to the subject without representing its actual appearance: vertical greens for trees, horizontal blues for the sea.

A realistic subject can also be reduced to a few geometric shapes: circles and triangles for trees, squares and rectangles for buildings. Combine several small shapes to make large ones. Arrange the geometric shapes in an interesting composition that suggests a landscape.

Quite often one abstraction leads to another and a series is born. Stay with a series until you find out where it is going. The process of abstraction is like the metamorphosis of caterpillar to butterfly, when the changes that take place may lead to a result that bears little resemblance to the original subject.

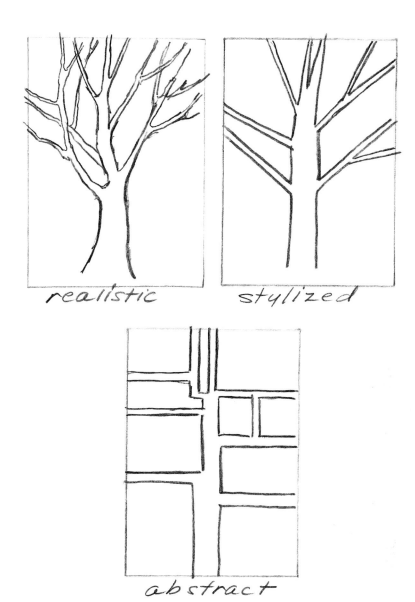

Realistic, stylized, abstract—you can move from one style to another as you explore creative possibilities.

Activity

Develop the abstraction of trees mentioned above a bit further, in two or three sketches. Place emphasis on a dominant element in each sketch, for example:
- —Emphasize the lacy, linear quality of the branches.
- —Develop large, blocky shapes—the "essence" of tree trunks.
- —Use expressive color, imaginary patterns.
- —Experiment with different directional movements: vertical, horizontal, diagonal.
- —Make the abstraction "threatening" or "inviting" or simply "fun."

You're not making a picture of a tree. This is the evolution of an abstract design beginning with the natural aspects of a tree. Almost any subject can be abstracted this way.

Abstraction to Realism

Abstraction is a two-way street. Not only can you start with a realistic image and abstract it, you can also create an abstract design and fit nature to it. It could turn out to be a landscape, a floral, a portrait, a still life. Flow paint or make marks until a realistic image takes shape. Your unconscious, packed with all of your experiences and ideas, directs the apparently accidental effects on your paper or canvas until you finally see what is there! This is a good way to use your visualization skills and imagination.

Set some limits. Since you are not restricted to a realistic subject, you can select an unusual size or format and work out a creative color scheme. Start with big, abstract shapes or gestural marks, arranging them on the support with an eye on the overall division of space. Pause occasionally to look for any suggestion of a subject: a spattered area that looks like weeds, a red splotch that suggests a cock's comb, a hidden face or figure. As the abstract develops, focus on what is happening in the picture. The original abstract design is just a place to start. If an image suggests itself, move in that direction. Be subtle; suggest rather than insist. Let your viewer discover the image.

Use the spontaneous method as a warm-up to get your creativity flowing, then put aside the unfinished abstract for another day if the images don't reveal themselves. Rotate the paper or canvas occasionally and study it from different directions to see what's there. Add another mark or shape to change the relationships and get things moving.

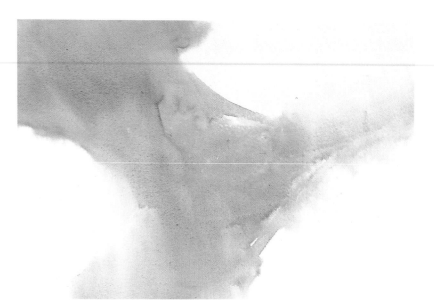

Stage 1. From a page of abstract design sketches, I selected one shape to flow over the paper in a limited palette, beginning with a mental picture of a bird in flight.

Stage 1. From a page of abstract design sketches, I selected one shape to flow over the paper in a limited palette, beginning with a mental picture of a bird in flight.

Activity

Fit a realistic subject into a geometric design. First design the geometric shapes, then abstract a subject from your imagination. Turn squares and rectangles into a cityscape, circles and ovals into flowers, triangles into a pine forest. Then turn a geometric abstract into a realistic image.

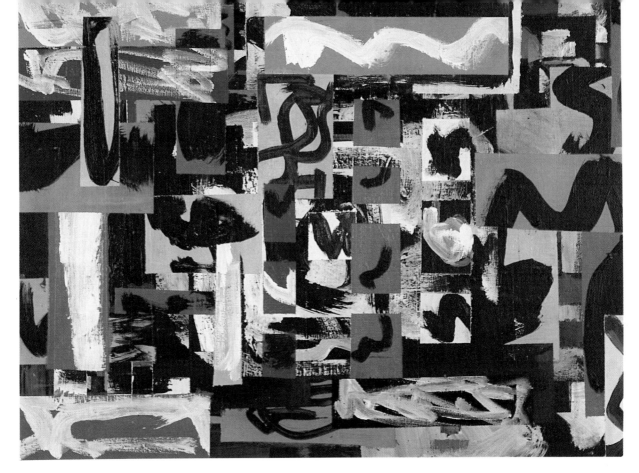

Abstracting Feelings

Artists express strong feelings with abstraction. Look at art reproductions in magazines and books to see how they do it: bold, angry brushstrokes, violent color, aggressive lines represent tremendous energy and expressive emotion. This energy is channeled through the artist's knowledge of art principles to emerge as a powerful statement of feeling.

Not all creative art is beautiful and pleasing to look at. Imagine abstracting your feelings from a headline in the newspaper about a tragic disaster or a monstrous act of terrorism. Expressionist paintings probing the depths of the human psyche are filled with anxiety and pain. Many of these abstract works have figurative subject matter or graphic symbols that are recognizable. Some express an intangible emotion through gesture, color, and other elements of design.

Inspired by his friend's colorful "surfer shorts," Finkel proclaims friendship, amusement, and delight in this painting. Even without the title you can sense the positive energy of his feelings in the exuberant color and bold gestural strokes. *New Wave Hal* by Bill Finkel. Acrylic, 18" x 24".

Activity

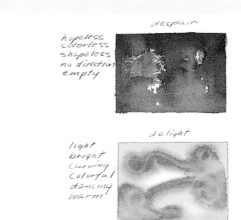

Try abstract expression. Make a picture without any reference to a real object. Think of a strong emotion: love, hate, rage, fear, ecstasy. Write down words that describe the feeling. Decide what will dominate your picture: jagged line, intense color. Would repetition be useful? Rhythm? Gradation? Design an abstract based on the emotion. For example, fury: red-orange, blue-purple, zig-zag, helter-skelter, slash-bash, vertical-diagonal, out-of-control.

Work out your design plan in a small color sketch, then enlarge it into a picture. You can do it!

Design for Design's Sake

Some abstract art is nonfigurative with no apparent reference to objects in the real world or to emotional expression. It comes in several forms: *optical art* uses color and value to create illusions of light and movement; *color-field* relies on color relationships for visual effect of floating or vibrating color; and *geometric design* emphasizes shape. This type of art is primarily rational and analytical, but artists rarely make art that is completely unemotional, so distinctions are often unclear.

Here the elements of design are the subject of the picture. Color for its own sake; line or pattern as the theme. Artists who work in this manner sometimes create ambiguous space with optical illusions suggesting light or the movement of geometric shapes. A picture may contain a combination of design factors, deriving its impact from the dominance of one of the elements, which is the "subject" of the picture.

This is a particular favorite of mine. The wonderful balance of complementary colors appeals to me visually. The shapes and textures seem "just right" when studied analytically, so I can enjoy the picture without concern for hidden meanings. This doesn't mean they aren't there—only that my response to the painting doesn't depend on them to be successful. *Fulani* by Virginia Lee Williams. Sand, modeling paste, gel medium, acrylic paint, 18" x 14".

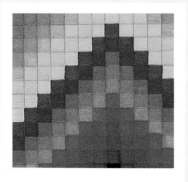

Activities

• Design a picture based on a simple one-half inch grid drawn on a six-inch square. Color each section with different values of a single color or use gradation to make the colors change gradually from section to section. Create a design different from mine, shown at left, using color and contrast to move the viewer's eye around the square.

• Make an abstract design of geometric shapes in pure hues. Unify the design through shape or color dominance. Enhance with line or texture. Try circles, triangles, and rectangles, with circles being the dominant shape and variations of blue as the dominant color, accented by a complementary orange. Then repeat the circular emphasis with a pattern of polka dots in a couple of areas to contrast with the flat colors. Playing with design this way strengthens your grip on all design factors, whether you are a realist or abstractionist.

Planning an Abstract

Abstract art uses many combinations of design factors. You can never exhaust the material for creative abstraction. You can keep from getting confused and still make abstract designs that are unique and personal by planning.

Abstract art is more than throwing paint or having an artistic tantrum on canvas or paper. Expressive art needs control. The power of a work of art comes from your ability to shape the raw energy of your original concept into pictorial form.

Define your problem, set boundaries for your creativity, and then push the boundaries to the limit! Decide the theme, the size of your artwork, the medium. Determine the design emphasis—line, shape, color, or value. Give yourself a time limit—one hour for this picture or ten variations in three hours. Now you're free to paint or draw spontaneously and creatively!

The elements and principles of design are absolutely essential to the organization of a good abstract picture. They help you get started and keep things from getting out of hand. Design points you in the right direction, but you can change that direction to suit your purpose. You can make, break, and modify the rules of the road.

Improvise, elaborate, exaggerate! You can design abstracts in a series, changing your emphasis each time. The more you do, the easier it gets. Make a checklist of the design fundamentals in Chapter Three and refer to it often until they come as second nature.

Start out with simple mediums you feel comfortable with: pencil, charcoal, pen and ink, colored pencil, marker, or crayon. Use typing paper or newsprint and lots of it. Add any other mediums or surfaces you like.

A design of the size and scope of this one doesn't just "happen." It calls for artistic control every step of the way. *Ancestral Spirit Dance #143* by Willis Bing Davis. 1988. Oil pastel, 40" x 60".

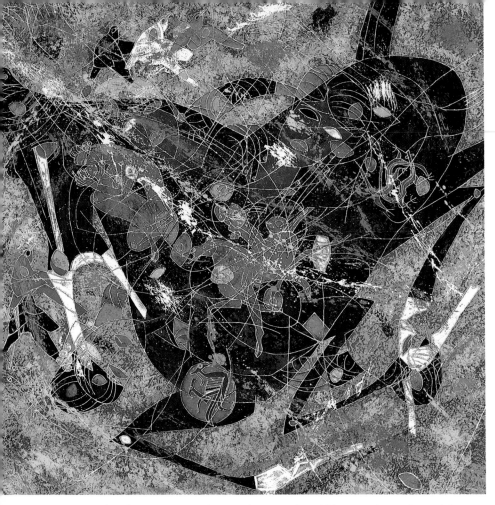

Design Fundamentals

Let's explore how to use the basic elements of design in creating abstract art and compare this to their use in realistic paintings.

Line

Abstract expressionist Hans Hofmann described line as "the direct flow of the personality into the work." Line is flexible, adaptable, changeable, a "plastic weapon with which to invent new forms." Hofmann felt line to be "one of the twentieth century's greatest formal inventions." Of course, line has had a principal role in defining shapes since the beginning of art, but only recently has line been used as the primary subject. The gestural line is emotional, the controlled line is rational. Pay attention to the quality of line: lyrical or dancing, aggressive or gentle.

What first appears to be simply textural scribbling on the surface of this painting is revealed on closer scrutiny to be figurative. There are faces and symbols that move the image closer to abstraction than the representation of the horse alone would be. *Black Horse* by Jiang Tiefeng. Mixed media on handmade rice paper, 41" x 41". Courtesy of Fingerhut Group Publishers, Inc.

Activity

Use free gestural line to begin an abstraction. Make a "scribble page" on ordinary bond paper. Start moving your pen, pencil, or charcoal slowly around the page, staying in contact with the paper at all times. Increase the pressure and speed. Don't think about a subject or about a picture, just keep the pencil moving. Let your unconscious mind draw the picture. Do two or three scribble drawings, then select a section of one to develop into a gestural abstraction. Erase, blend, or darken areas to create gradation of values and textural changes, enhancing the quality of line that is peculiar to the drawing.

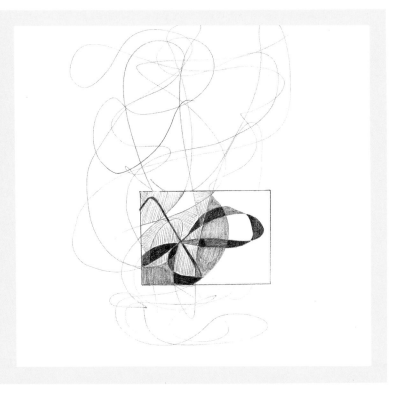

A free, gestural line is a good way to begin an abstraction.

Shape

You have more latitude in the arrangement of shapes in an abstract picture than in an image representing reality. In the realistic picture, you can make only minor adjustments to the shapes of the subject without risking the integrity of the image. In the abstract picture, you can take liberties with the image, distorting, exaggerating, even losing it entirely. Simplify and arrange shapes creatively to make a visually interesting abstract design.

Still life shapes are superimposed on scribbles of white wax crayon. One of Beam's favorite characters—the cat with pointed ears—appears when the washes are applied. The invisible drawing holds the picture together, along with a white shape bordered by middle darks. I like Beam's daring to place the blue strawberries in the corner—a deliberate breaking of the rules that works because of the blue shape at the top, which keeps the berries from rolling out of the picture. *Green Smiles and Blue Strawberries* by Mary Todd Beam. Mixed media resist, 30" x 40"

Activity

Make value drawings of individual still life objects using different viewpoints and light sources: a pitcher, a cup and saucer, a glass, a plate, some fruit and vegetables. Distort the forms if you like. Cut up the sketches, following the value changes on the surface of the objects. Assemble the pieces in fractured planes of light and dark, using only the pieces that aid the design. Unify the design with line, enhanced values, or texture.

Use a value drawing of still life objects, cut into pieces according to values, to construct an abstract like this one.

Keirns has taken an unusual color approach to her abstraction, suggestive of flowing water. A water theme is usually painted in cool colors. She has charged the design with energy by using warm hues. *Downstream* by Lyn Keirns. Watercolor, 20" x 25". Collection of Mr. and Mrs. Vincent Bednor, Columbus, Ohio.

Here the red is aggressively pushing itself into the foreground. Try to imagine the composition with a cool blue or green in that spot. What would happen to the dramatic color shock in the painting? *Rock Mosaic* by Alexander Nepote. Layered mixed media, 30" x 40".

Color

You have a "color personality" that has a powerful effect on the way you use color in your art. Learn which colors are right for you by exploring pigments and experimenting with mixtures. Be as whimsical or dramatic as you choose. Set your own boundaries. You can limit the number of pigments, pick a distinctive color scheme, or choose an unusual contrast effect. When you abstract a realistic subject, use creative color instead of local color (the real color of the objects).

In abstract pictures painted in pure hues, the brilliant color and shock of the color vibration give energy to the painting. Sometimes contrast pure hues with neutral gray or with a color that has been modified toward gray. They will seem more vivid, while the grays provide visual relief.

Create ambiguous spatial relationships by reversing the traditional order of receding cool colors and advancing warm colors.

Complementaries can provide strong color excitement in abstract pictures. When complements are side by side, they set up a vibration that makes the colors sing.

Activities
• Make an abstraction of landscape forms, changing the usual temperature, intensity, and value arrangements to flatten the picture space and create color vibration. Exaggerate the temperature and intensity differences.

• Make an abstract picture using seven to ten overlapping shapes and flat, pure hues. Repeat shapes with variations in size and hue, using color, value, and temperature contrast to energize the shapes. Make a "hole" in the design with extreme contrast of value or color.

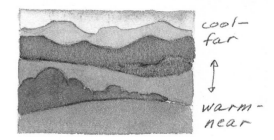

Reverse the usual arrangement of warm and cool colors.

Experiment with overlapping forms to learn how to use color, value, and temperature in new and different ways.

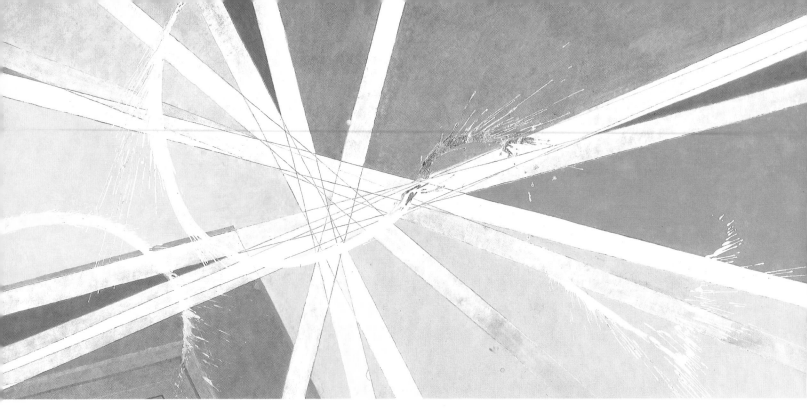

This painting hardly needs explanation in terms of its expression of tension and energy. I might, however, mention that I recall Bradshaw saying in a workshop, "Whatever you do, do it with conviction!" He clearly follows his own good counsel. *Counterplay I* by Glenn R. Bradshaw. Casein on rice paper, 37" x 73". Corporately owned.

Tension/Energy

You can create tension and energy in your abstract picture through manipulation of lines, shapes, colors, repetition, rhythm, and gradation. Use line quality to create movement, suggesting energy, action, and speed. Reinforce that sense of movement in the colors and shapes through gradation, repetition, and rhythm.

Activity

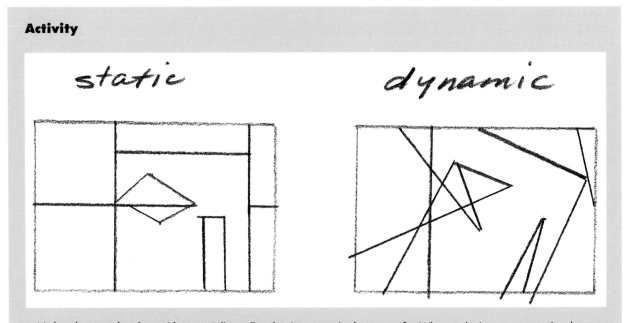

Make abstract sketches with energy lines. Emphasize a particular type of movement or direction— static, flowing, or rhythmic. Enhance the movement with gradations of color, size, and value, changing hues from warm to cool, pure to dull, or light to dark. Create tension by changing direction and color.

When a design seems static, change the line and shapes to make it more dynamic.

Patterns/Textures

The patterns of nature are wonderfully adaptable to abstract design: Make use of the patterns in microscopic views of organisms, in cross-sections of fruits and vegetables, in rocks and shells, in sponges.

The man-made environment and mechanical objects afford additional opportunities for abstraction: brick or stone walls, stacked objects, machinery, tools, and gears. These are excellent starting places for abstract art.

Whatever exists in nature is there for you. Shape it with artistic intent; show the naturalistic origin if you wish or leave the real behind. *Bisti Wilderness* by Virginia Cobb. Watercolor, ink, charcoal, 22" x 30".

Activities

Make an abstraction based on natural patterns: rock strata, the inside of a nutshell, seashells, the veins in a leaf. Use variations of a pattern or texture, incorporate rhythm and gradation. Use dominance of color, shape, or value to resolve the composition as it becomes more complex.

Chapter 6
Experimentation: Exploring New Territory

"Creation is dominated by three absolutely different factors: first, nature, which works upon us by its laws; second, the artist, who creates a spiritual contact with nature and his materials; third, the medium of expression through which the artist translates his inner world."

Hans Hofmann, Search for the Real

A master of many complex mediums, Davis has used the simple materials of cut and torn paper collage for this stunning abstract. Yes, it takes experience and practice to create art as fine as this—but it doesn't take all that just to get started. *African Rain Forest #2* by Willis Bing Davis. 1988. Collage, 40" x 30". Collection of Paul Nelson.

Make your creative journey even more interesting and exciting—*venture into the unknown!* You don't have to wrack your brain thinking of something no one has ever heard of. Just do something you haven't done before. Paint with a gigantic brush, use your left hand, use both hands. Experimentation is simply getting into the creative mode by an unaccustomed route.

A couple of new colors, a few scribbles or marks with a different tool or medium—this is the way to start. Each touch of the brush or pencil, every added color changes relationships, brings up another idea. Action calls for response. You ask yourself, "Where does this want to go?" It doesn't matter if the outcome isn't a finished piece. "Art is an experience, not an object," said Robert Motherwell.

Experimenting brings your creative self to the surface. Experimenting makes you ask questions and search for solutions. When you change your medium or the way you handle your materials, your design emphasis changes as well. When you put down your pencil and pick up a brush, emphasis on color supersedes value. When you experiment with collage, shapes and pattern dominate. Every medium or tool has a distinctive "look," which becomes even more distinctive in the hands of different artists.

As you experiment, continue to use the design fundamentals. Sharpen your observational skills by drawing. Keep your journal up to date, describing mediums and techniques. Brainstorm new combinations of mediums. Look for ideas in this book.

The variety of art materials is awe-inspiring—and so is the cost! Don't change too many things at once. Trade a few supplies with artist friends; dust off those items you bought for a workshop and never used. Or buy three new tubes of paint, six pastel sticks, three different sheets of paper.

No medium or method is "better" than another; they are only different. Each has advantages for the creative artist. You probably have your own favorites. Pencil, crayons, chalk, finger paints, and other materials you used as a child allow you to relax and have fun with your art. Mixed mediums offer the challenge of change. Consider the possibilities!

The important thing is to begin. This is an adventure— open your mind to creativity and make things happen!

Somehow you have to get that first mark on blank paper or canvas. Using materials you already have, prepare surfaces for painting or drawing and set them aside. A prepared sheet is usually more inviting than a blank one. Getting the supports ready is a creative experience in itself.

By limiting herself to a single subject—cows—Stolzenberger is free to explore a great variety of interpretations of that subject. Mixing mediums and paper surfaces is a great way to experiment. The artist has created an abstract design with her realistic subject matter. *Remnants of a Ruminant's Ruminations* by Sharon L. Stolzenberger. Watercolor, ink, pencil, collage, 28" x 36".

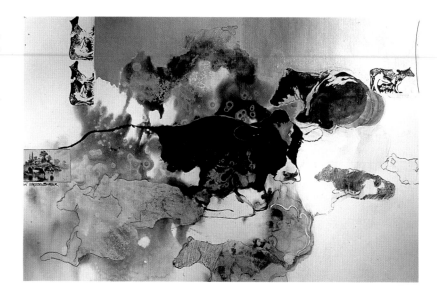

Activities

Here are some things you can do to prepare paper, board, or canvas for later use. Make three or four of these supports and start your next picture with one of them.

• Make rubbings on paper or unstretched canvas from textured surfaces: string, leaves, weeds, coins, fabric, or screen. Scribble random marks and graffiti in light pencil. Or use white crayon or paraffin to make invisible marks that will resist water mediums. Scratch, crumple, fold, bend, scribble, tear, or patch the surface of the supports.

• Glue layers of rice paper, wrapping tissue, torn drawings, or watercolors on paper, illustration board, or canvas using a solution of 50 percent water and 50 percent white glue or acrylic matte medium.

• Squeeze, drip, spatter, or paint gesso with brush or brayer on heavy paper, board, or canvas. Establish a dominant line, direction, or pattern. Sprinkle sand in it. Drag a comb through it.

• Stain paper or canvas with thin washes of light-fast inks, acrylic, or watercolor. Use as a toned support, as the beginning of a color design or as collage papers.

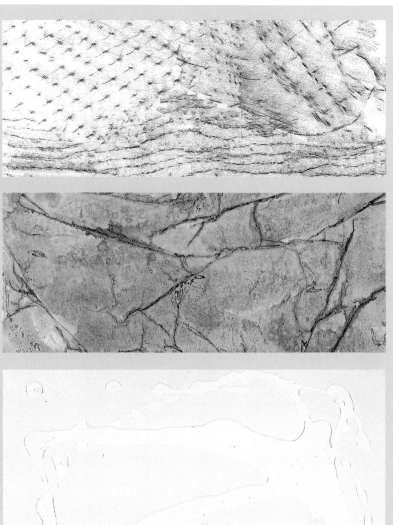

Play around with your materials. Try using rubbings, rice paper overlays, or dripped gesso.

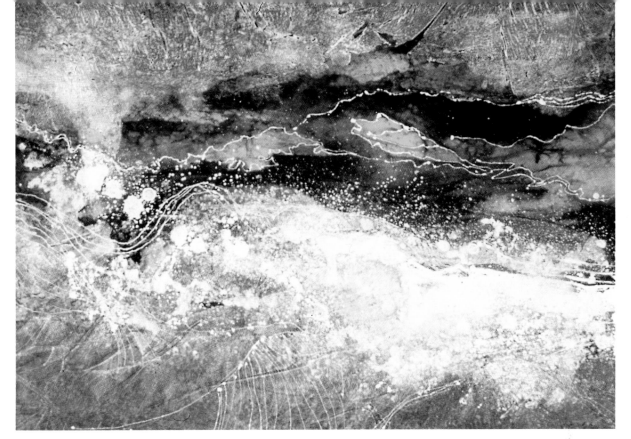

Stay with a picture as long as you can still find something to learn from it. Some papers can be peeled off in layers while they're wet, revealing a white, rough texture or spots and stains that have soaked through from the top layer. This may help you get started in another direction as it did for me in this picture. *Tidal Surge* by Nita Leland. Inks, collage, 18" x 24". Private collection.

Be Ready for Adventure

Experimentation is a vital component of the creative process. There are probably a great many things you haven't attempted yet. You don't need to accomplish something that has never been done in the history of art. There isn't much that is really new.

Try something different, even though it feels a bit awkward at first. Technical virtuosity alone doesn't make an expressive painting. Art that is "slick" impresses people, but it doesn't necessarily move them. Most people prefer sincerity to glibness. When you have something to say and are having fun saying it, it shows in the work. *So get out there and play!*

Give each new medium, tool, or technique a chance. Don't be intimidated by materials. Work quickly, spontaneously, and confidently. Do many small "samples" of an experiment. Your unconscious mind will do some of the work for you. The key words are *relaxed control*.

You have an affinity for some mediums and others may leave you cold. You'll find out what your preferences are as you work—and you may even be surprised! Experience and practice give you the confidence to invent and innovate. Use materials you enjoy working with, but don't settle on one too soon.

As you try new things, take notes in your journal for future use. That way, when you create a fantastic effect with a unique combination of materials, you'll be able to remember how you did it.

Once you begin to experiment, keep moving! Change a technique, a tool, a surface— not all at once, but often enough to keep it interesting. Make a "trial run" with the new materials before starting a painting. Turn off your judgmental, critical left brain as you work and let your right brain take over. Encourage yourself to work quickly, more quickly than you can think. Set a time limit: ten minutes for a watercolor, three drawings in fifteen minutes. *Don't keep telling yourself what to do—simply do.* Save evaluation for later, so you don't interrupt the creative flow. Enjoy the process. Make fewer critical demands on yourself when you're trying something new, and have some fun with it.

When you're ready to critique your work, take a positive approach by listing all of the things you like about the piece. In your next experiment, use the things that worked.

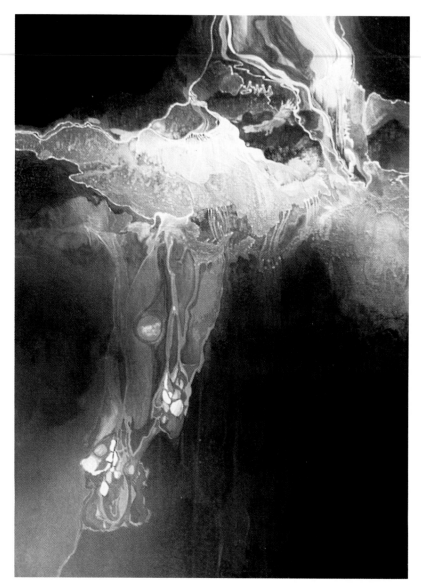

Rothermel combines the best of both worlds in her sensitive paintings: intellect and intuition. However spontaneously a picture may begin, she will zero in on a "happening" and resolve it into a cohesive design. *Haforn* by Joan Ashley Rothermel. Watermedia, 29" x 20".

Follow Your Impulses

A lot of workshops emphasize flashy techniques, but little is said about structure and control. Hoping to become more spontaneous and free, students throw or flow paint with abandon and pray something will "happen." After all, the demo looked so easy! Don't forget—the instructor has done this many times. Experience makes the demonstration look spontaneous.

In experimental painting you need freedom to explore. You don't want to have an inflexible plan, but do have a general idea of what your objective is. Consider your concept, choose a format, develop a basic design plan, determine a focal point, plan color, decide on medium and technique. These are the "limitations" that circumscribe your creative quest. Maintain flexibility, adapt to the unexpected, force change as you experiment. *Move back and forth freely between plan and impulse.*

It's fun to spatter or flow paint as an underpainting and develop a concept from the design that results. Searching for image and design in the rela-tionships on the page boosts your skills in visualizing. Every beginning has possibilities. Some people determine the concept at the outset; for others it takes shape as the work progresses. Through the process of elimination, correction, and realignment, you shape the picture to fit your concept. Without the concept and your control over the design, the piece is just an accident, happy or otherwise. Don't stop at the "happy accident" when you are making art. Resolve the composition. Direct your creativity. Take control.

Activities

• Look for accidental designs in random ink lines and shapes. Dip a piece of damp twine in India ink and doodle it or drop it on a sheet of paper or 3" x 5" card. Extend the linear design with pen or brush, or delete some lines with opaque white. Create shapes where the lines suggest them.

• Spatter a few drops of ink on typing paper or a card. Blow through a drinking straw to move the ink around, turning the paper as you blow. Develop the design that forms in the network of lines, adding lines and shapes or blocking out with opaque white.

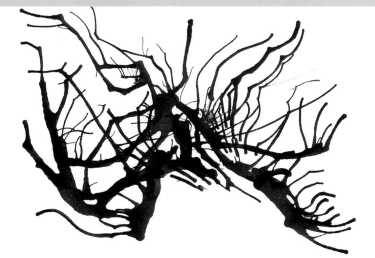

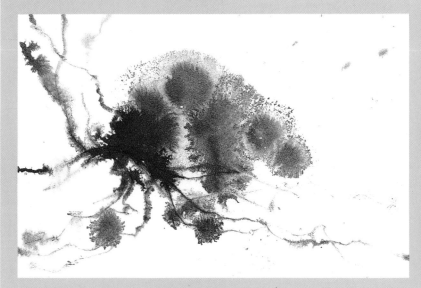

• Dampen or spatter smooth, medium weight paper with clear water. Drop or spatter ink on the damp sheet and let it spread. Draw through the wet areas with a stick or brush dipped in ink. Add shapes and lines to make an abstract design, and connect some areas to the edges. If you see a realistic image, develop it. Save these experiments for your collage box.

Ink lends itself to creative experimenting. Explore the potential of string dipped in ink, blowing ink through a straw, or flowing ink on damp paper.

As a rule, artists don't shop at craft stores, but you'd be surprised at all the goodies you can find there. I was so intrigued by the Guatemalan worry dolls—tell them your troubles and they'll take them away for you—that I put them in this painting. The pom-poms and glitter came from the craft shop, too, along with a few other curiosities I haven't used yet. Was it fun making this painting? You bet! *Fiesta* by Nita Leland. Watercolor, collage, pom-poms, glitter, worry dolls, 22" x 30".

Trailblazing

Sometimes when you want to be a pioneer in the wilderness, you discover that someone else has already been there. That's all right. What you do will be different.

Learn the limitations and advantages of mediums. Each has unique qualities. Find out what these are. You use a particular medium because it "feels right" to you, but have you explored its creative possibilities? You might switch to an unfamiliar medium to challenge yourself or satisfy your curiosity. You can combine mediums to realize greater potential from both.

Do a little detective work. Which mediums are compatible? How do other artists use them? What you learn is a point of departure for your experimentation. There is no substitute for your own experience with a medium. Play with tools, explore pigments, learn by doing.

Don't be surprised if you suddenly feel like sewing buttons on the canvas or cutting up your watercolors and weaving them together. Do it! When you're thinking creatively you come up with some pretty unusual ideas. Give new ideas a chance!

When you're getting serious about a medium, use the finest materials you can afford. Artists' pigments are more brilliant than student colors. Good canvas and paper make more durable supports. You want a finished piece to be made with quality materials.

Mediums and Techniques

In experimental work the lines between painting, drawing, and printmaking are blurred. Some techniques incorporate all three in the same picture. A lot of latitude is permitted in the combinations of mediums, as long as the materials you use together won't make the picture self-destruct! Your library has books that cover compatibility and safe use of art materials, so when in doubt, look it up. Here are some of the mediums and techniques that can be used in the activities that follow:

finger paints	gouache
pencils	casein
crayons	acrylics
pastels, chalk	oil paint
oil pastels	alkyds
charcoal	ink resist
conté crayon	collage
graphite	transfer
markers	printing
light-fast ink	monotype
watercolor	stencils

Start with the mediums you have or can easily acquire and see how far you can go with them. The support you work on will depend on the mediums you choose. Some of the possibilities are:

watercolor paper or board
rice paper
pastel paper
illustration board
printmaking paper
drawing paper
canvas and canvas board
fabric
untempered Masonite
wood panel

Activity

Finger painting isn't just for kids. This is a great way to loosen yourself up, to play with paint and color. Buy finger paint ready-made in an art or school supply store. Put a couple of blobs of paint on a smooth support. Finger painting paper is specially treated, but you can also use smooth cardboard, newsprint, illustration board, hot press watercolor paper, or smooth cardboard. Spread it around with your hands, a flat painting knife, spatula, or credit card. Make marks with your fingers, your palm, a comb, a sponge; draw in the paint with a brush handle, a butter knife, or a cotton swab. Drop a sheet of paper on top of your finger painting and press it smooth, then pull it off and you'll have a print. Save these "masterpieces" for the collage box.

Finger paint is a great way to get back in touch with your childlike spontaneity and the unadulterated joy of creation. Try using a palette knife or creating prints.

Add your own ideas. Combine paper and fabric, fabric and wood. Dig into your treasure and collage boxes for odds and ends to add. Work from designs in your sketchbook/ journal or start spontaneously on one of your prepared supports. Limit yourself to a couple of new elements to begin with. It doesn't take much to start the ball rolling.

Read through this chapter to get a feel for some of the possibilities. Keep track of new ideas that pop into your head, and write them down before they go away. You'll be glad you did. Then return to the activities you want to do and jump right in! Make lots of sample sheets with the new techniques. Then use them in your pictures.

Drawing Mediums

You can go beyond line and tone if drawing is your first love. Contemporary artists use expressive gesture and color in drawings. Use the lowly crayon, or make a drawing with brush and watercolor, oils, or acrylics. Resist and transfer drawing are intriguing variations of drawing techniques. Mixing mediums is absolutely acceptable.

Shunk soaks a picture from an old magazine or newspaper in lacquer thinner, places it on his paper, then rubs the back to transfer the image. Experiment to find the right combination of materials. Some inks and solvents don't work as well as others. (If you use solvents, pay special attention to ventilation in your workplace.) Once you've completed the transfer process, you can incorporate other drawing techniques and mediums to develop a balanced composition. *Cézanne's Apples* by Hal Shunk. Transfer drawing with pastel, 30" x 22".

Activities
- Combine wet and dry mediums in a drawing on illustration board or heavy paper. Make an abstract or a realistic drawing in charcoal or soft pencil and spray lightly with fixative. Let it dry, then flow transparent ink or watercolor washes over the lines. Add pattern and value in colored pencil.
- Make a random line resist drawing with wax crayon or paraffin. Flow on ink or watercolor washes. When the washes are dry, add colored pencil lines and patterns.
- Draw with watercolor pencils or water soluble crayons on damp paper to produce blurred lines and tints. Add watercolor washes.

Combine wet and dry mediums, create a crayon resist with watercolor and add colored pencil, or use watercolor pencil on damp paper.

Pastels

When working with pastels, you can layer one color over another. Use any paper with "tooth," including charcoal or pastel paper, watercolor paper, and specially prepared sand-finished papers. Pastel may be applied light over dark with or without blending. Add lines with vine charcoal or ink. Pastel can also be used to add surface patterns to a watercolor.

Oil pastel sticks have a heavy binder that is soluble in mineral spirits or turpentine. Blend oil pastels with brush and turps for a painterly handling, or dampen the surface with turpentine and draw directly into the damp surface. Use oil pastels on dry oil paintings, adding line and patterns.

Oil pastel is a painting medium in Davis's hands, yet at the same time the gestural line has the quality of a drawing. Combined in this powerful painting, they make a vibrant affirmation of Davis's proud commitment to the theme of his ancestral heritage. *Ancestral Spirit Dance #115* by Willis Bing Davis. 1987. Oil pastel, 40" x 64". Collection of Bill and Camille Cosby.

Chalk-like pastel can be worked into the paper, heavily layered or scumbled as shown in the reclining figure, allowing the color of the paper to show through.

Watercolor, Gouache, and Casein

The flow of the paint and the white paper glimmering through transparent washes are unique to transparent watercolor. The purist relies on creative design schemes rather than experimental techniques, but if you have a mind to play with watercolor, almost anything goes! Watercolor may be combined with many drawing and water-based mediums and applied to a variety of surfaces besides traditional watercolor papers. Use hot press watercolor paper, clay-coated drawing paper, or gesso-prepared surfaces for different effects.

Gouache and casein are opaque watercolors, both compatible with other water-based mediums, although casein dries to a hard film, unlike watercolor and gouache. An opaque medium may be applied light over dark because of

Gouache is well suited to the controlled pointillist technique. Cain uses dots of pure color that appear blended when the viewer stands back from the painting. *Red Plums* by Karen Cain. Acrylic gouache, 18" x 24".

its density and covering power. Gouache and casein make elegant, translucent glazes. The dense pigment also works well in printing techniques.

Whatever special effects you use to enhance the surface appearance of a watercolor, begin with a creative concept and a sturdy design structure.

Bradshaw works casein into both sides of the rice paper until he determines which side will develop into the better design. From that point he works on one side only until the painting is completed. Since casein is an opaque medium, light colors may be placed over dark or the paint may be thinned to make translucent glazes. *Tracks and Traces* by Glenn R. Bradshaw. Casein on rice paper, 37" x 73". Corporately owned.

Activities

• Make a resist "sampler," using resists and frisket with water-based mediums to texturize or reserve white areas. Use tape and "stick-ons" for hard edge designs. Some possibilities: rubber cement, liquid frisket, paraffin, wax crayon, colored wax pencils, waxed paper, masking and drafting tapes, dots, and labels. Apply the resist and let it dry, then apply watercolor washes. Rub off the frisket or cement, add glazes, or emphasize white areas with dark lines.

• Paint an object with gouache or casein mixed with watercolor. Place the object on paper and lay another sheet of paper on top. Roll a brayer over this sandwich to make a print. Try a sponge, tissue, paper towel, crumpled foil, leaves, burlap, or lace, and incorporate the printed texture into a design.

• Stencils can be used to create unity and rhythm through the repetition of a shape. Vary the shape occasionally, changing its size and the spaces between the shapes. Cut stencils representing figures, flowers, leaves, or geometric shapes from heavy paper. Sponge out areas of a watercolor using the stencil pattern; paint or spatter into the stencil design.

• Make a small ink painting on paper or board using vivid, waterproof colors. Block out color and white areas with white gouache and let dry. Then paint over the picture with black India ink. When the ink is dry, gently wash the ink and gouache off under cool running water.

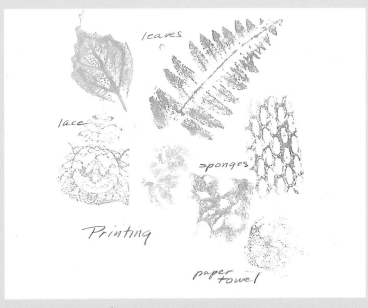

Find new ways to work with familiar mediums, such as resists, prints, and stencils.

Acrylics

Water-based acrylic paints are adaptable to both transparent and opaque techniques. They adhere to almost any clean surface that isn't oily and may be used as underpainting for oils. Don't paint *over* oil paint with acrylics, however. Use canvas, watercolor paper, and illustration boards as they come or coated with gesso. Change the density and flow

When many elements are combined in experimental painting, acrylics are the solution to many problems. Layers dry quickly, the medium adheres solidly, tools clean up easily in water, and many other mediums are compatible with acrylics. This award-winning painting was done on stretched watercolor paper. *Secret Chamber I* by Carole Myers, N.W.S. Acrylic collage on paper, 29" x 21".

Activities

• Pour a thin layer of gloss medium onto a piece of glass, letting it spread into an organic shape six to eight inches across. Drop colored inks or fluid acrylics into the medium and stir the color lightly with a brush handle. When the medium is dry, peel it off and adhere it to a white support with gel medium. Combine several of these small panels. Leave the background white or create a free-form stained glass effect by painting dark lines between the colored panels.

• Spread a thick mixture of acrylic gel or modeling paste and acrylic matte medium on heavy paper or board. In the wet mix print textures of sponges, cutouts, corrugated cardboard, leaves, string—anything that will leave an imprint. Let the mixture dry. Paint the textured surface with acrylics. For a unified painting, decide on a theme and a basic design plan before you begin and make your textured foundation support your concept.

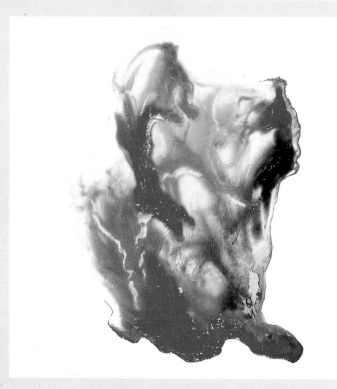

Pour and peel—it's as easy as that.

of the paint by adding gel medium to thicken and make it transparent or by mixing the paint with modeling paste for a sculptural quality. Control the finish by adding glossy or matte polymer mediums. Add iridescent acrylic colors for beautiful color effects. Acrylics dry very quickly, so you can paint without interrupting your creative flow. (Tip: Squeeze tube acrylics onto a dampened, folded paper towel on the palette to keep them workable longer.)

Collage and Assemblage

Some of the most creative art done today is collage, partly owing to the versatility and durability of acrylic mediums. The materials used in collage are virtually unlimited, with one caution: The support must be heavy enough to bear the weight of the material to be applied. Supports include canvas, untempered Masonite, watercolor paper and board, and illustration board. Collage and assemblage materials consist of papers of all weights, shapes, textures, and colors; "found" papers such as tickets, candy wrappers, cancelled stamps, posters; silk-screened papers; marbled papers; metallic foils; newspapers; photos; string; fabrics; wire; mirrors—just about anything your imagination can conjure up and your ingenuity can unearth. Materials may be torn, cut, crumpled, tangled, or mashed. The finished piece may be flat or decidedly three-dimensional. Use white polymer glue diluted 50 percent with water for flat pieces. Spread gel medium on three-dimensional objects and imbed them in more medium on the support. For extremely heavy pieces, use epoxy glue.

This many-layered piece is almost sculptural in places. Williams recommends coating heavier objects with acrylic gel and imbedding them in modeling paste for a secure attachment to the support. *and to the jewels of the sea* by Virginia Lee Williams. Torn papers, acrylic paint, iridescent plastic film, 26″ x 35″.

Painted papers, torn, pleated and folded, are the basis for this interesting horizontal arrangement on a vertical format. The torn edge of the paper introduces a linear element. As an interesting aside, let me tell you about motivation to create: Webb broke her right wrist several years ago and couldn't paint, so she worked with her left hand, soaking and crumpling papers for collage. That's the kind of spirit that drives creativity! *Ligne* by Judith Webb. Mixed media, 38″ x 30″.

Collage is a form that seems to encourage creativity. You can use a theme, as in this nature collage, or combine diverse elements.

Activities

• Add sand, leaves, twigs, weeds, string, yarn, thread, stone chips, bits of glass, or tiny sea shells to acrylic gel medium and design a picture around the fragments, using the "bits and pieces" as the start of a theme for your picture.

• Start with a "color idea," an expressive, unique color combination. Tone several pieces of heavy paper with colored ink, watercolor, or acrylic washes, using the colors you have chosen. Tear the paper into pieces with interesting shapes and ar- range the pieces into a composition, using some of the torn edges as white lines between the shapes. Add other papers from your collage box or tinted rice papers for pattern and contrast. Glue the papers down with white polymer glue.

• Paint an abstract design in ink or watercolor on paper, or acrylic on canvas or paper. Layer torn rice pa- per or white wrapping tissue over some areas using a 50-50 solution of white glue or matte medium and wa- ter. Glaze and layer alternately to create your design.

Color ties together this torn paper collage.

Acrylic and rice paper lend them- selves to an abstract collage.

Change

While you're experimenting with mediums, continue to invite creativity in other ways as well. For example, rearrange the furniture in your art space, so you're facing a different direction. Instead of sitting down to paint or draw, stand up. Paint at a different time of day or paint with a group, instead of alone.

Whatever you're doing now, consider how you might do it differently. Usually, it's habit that stifles your artistic impulses. If I had to summarize in one word how to stimulate creativity, that word would be *change*.

Activity

• Make a drawing or painting using both hands at once. For instance, hold a pencil in each hand and do a gesture drawing. Do the marks you made with the hand you use less have a different quality?

• Do sketches of people or animals, using colored markers to experiment with color. Try the outrageous —purple hair, orange eyes— to see what effects you can create.

• Start a picture using touch instead of sight. Arrange your materials for easy access, then close your eyes and block in the basic design. Finish the painting with your eyes open, but don't change the design.

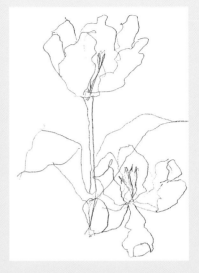

Drawing with a pencil in each hand can create interesting line quality, as in this sketch of a flower.

Use unusual colors to express something unique about your subject.

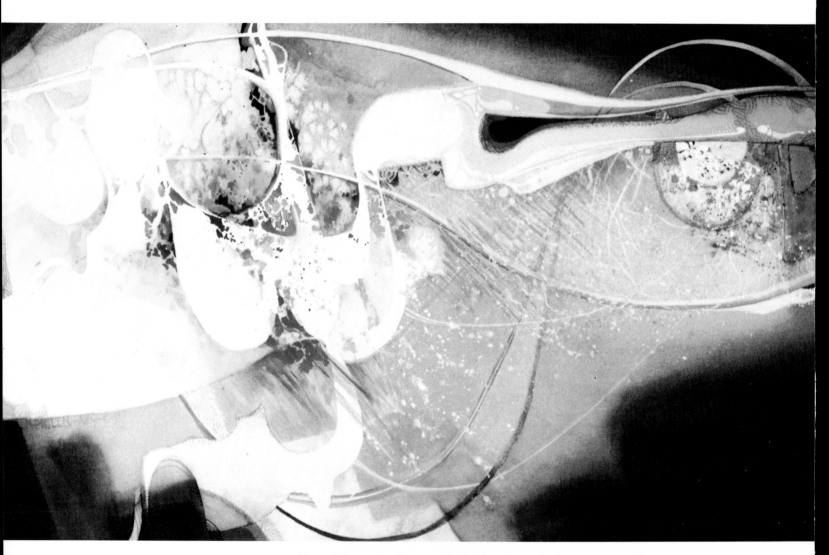

The swiftly moving lines and intriguing shapes in this painting make me
think of space and time, of other realities, of infinite possibilities. The quest
for creativity in a painting such as this begins with risk-taking and ends with
a sense of completion—and an urgent need to begin yet another creative
adventure. *Galactic Connection* by Marilyn Hughey Phillis. © 1987. Watercolor, gouache,
rice paper collage, 12 ¼" x 19 ¼". Collection of the artist.

Chapter 7
The Great Adventure

"When the artist is alive in any person . . . he becomes an inventive, searching, daring, self-expressing creature. He becomes interesting to other people. He disturbs, upsets, enlightens, and he opens ways for a better understanding."

Robert Henri, The Art Spirit

Being an artist would be a lot easier if you weren't so hard on yourself. You are your own worst critic most of the time. When I critique student work in my classes, there are always a few students who say, "Tear this apart—tell me everything that's wrong with it. I know it's awful, but I can take it." Why should I do that, when I believe you can build on your strengths?

Look for the parts of the picture that "work." ***Learn from the things you do right.*** Keep doing these things again and again. The rest will shape up as you progress. You get a little

bit better every time you paint or draw, so the secret is to keep doing it as often as you can!

Your growth as a creative artist is greatly affected by your attitudes, both toward yourself and toward art in general. ***Respect the work of others, no matter how different it may be from your own.*** If the emotional content turns you off, look for design factors you can appreciate. If the design troubles you, see if you can figure out what the problem is. Don't just dismiss it. Learn as much as you can from it. Paul Jacques Grillo wrote in *Form, Function and Design*, "(T)he humblest work may possess eternal greatness if it possesses sincerity."

Your progress in art is in a direct ratio to the time you spend making art. Your temperament will determine to a great extent how quickly you progress. I have had students who painted every day between class sessions. Many of them are now professional artists. Others only painted in class—and they are still taking classes and enjoying it.

A simple statement, uncomplicated shapes, and pure, bright hues can suggest grandeur and elegance in a large-scale painting. Look at the picture upside down and sideways to appreciate the abstract design underlying the realistic image.
Untitled by Mel Meyer, S.M. Acrylic on canvas, 72" x 72".

Know why you want to paint or draw. Is it:

- a need for self-expression
- a desire to create beauty
- a wish to communicate
- an enjoyable, satisfying use of leisure time
- a means of making money
- a way to kill time?

There is no single "correct" answer to this question. The more interest and effort you put into art, the better your work will be. It's as simple as that. Every artist has bouts of uncertainty. Conquer self-doubt by practicing your skills. The less you have to worry about technique, the more expressive your art will become.

Take time to develop skills and awareness. A student watching 82-year-old Edgar Whitney demonstrate his watercolor skills whined, "Why can't I do it that easily?" Ed scowled at her and growled, "When you've been doing it for sixty years, maybe you will!" It doesn't take all of sixty years—but it does take time.

Be patient. Gustave Flaubert said, "Talent is long patience." That's what it takes to make art.

Making art is a wonderful experience, but it isn't always "easy." That's all right. Sometimes your best work comes out of a battle with a concept or an encounter with materials. *Don't avoid the struggle that produces meaningful art.*

If you're struggling, change something. Do whatever it takes to give you a fresh start. Switch mediums, tools, or techniques. Go outside to paint. Paint or draw at a different time of day. Modify your subject using one of the words in the list. Copy this list of "modifiers" in your

This striking watercolor is almost photographic, but Akers has chosen what to put in and leave out—something a camera can't do. *Orkney Summer* by Gary Akers. Watercolor, 17 ½" x 25".

sketchbook/journal and add a few words of your own:

add
combine
distort
divide
energize
exaggerate
fade
fracture
magnify
multiply
reduce
reverse
sharpen
soften
stretch
substitute
subtract

Use this list to inspire you when you approach a new painting.

Expect to have plateaus. Don't be discouraged when they occur. When you're stuck, refine your skills at that level. As your skills improve, introduce small changes—a new brush, a different pencil, an unusual color, an unexpected texture. Use this book for ideas to get you started again. Keep moving!

Nobody gets stuck forever!

Activity
What is the most boring subject cliché you can think of? I won't give you a hint, because your idea may be different from mine. Make the most exciting painting or drawing you can of this subject, using the list of modifiers to alter it. Remember: A picture doesn't have to be "beautiful," but it does have to say something about the subject through your use of design.

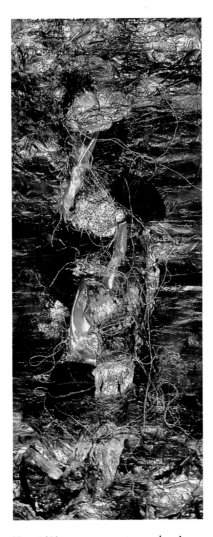

Huart-Wourms came to my beginning watercolor class several years ago. She showed me tiny fragments of handmade paper that looked like pretty little bits of nothing. She touched them like they were something wonderful. In time she learned the ancient art of papermaking. Now she stirs her creative spirit into every batch of paper pulp and exquisite pieces like *Golden Path* are made. *Golden Path* by R. Huart-Wourms. Handmade paper and metallic thread, 48" x 20".

Truth in Art

There ought to be a "truth in art" law, just as there is a requirement for truth in advertising. If there were, artists might be more tolerant of others' efforts to express what they believe to be true in their art. This law shouldn't establish standards for truth, but it should allow free rein to whatever the artist says as long as it is sincerely and honestly felt. *Trust your instincts above the advice or criticism of others —* especially when you feel you have expressed the truth in your art.

Georgia O'Keeffe wrote to her friend Anita Pollitzer,

I don't see why we ever think of what others think of what we do — no matter who they are. Isn't it enough just to express yourself?

Ben Shahn also questioned himself. "This may be art, but is it my own art?" and he went on to say,

. . . I began to realize that however professional my work might appear, even however original it might be, it still did not contain the central person which, for good or ill, was myself.

Finding the "central person" that is yourself is a worthwhile and necessary objective for every creative artist.

Art doesn't have to be "beautiful" to be art, as long as it is truthful to the artist's understanding and feelings about the world. A pretty picture may express one kind of truth for you, but that isn't the only truth there is. A picture may be a wrenching representation of human cruelty — not pretty, but a masterwork of artistic elements intelligently organized to express that terrible reality.

How does it happen that you occasionally do a picture that is beyond your present level of skills? This is a clue to your real potential! You were probably so absorbed that you overcame your self-consciousness as you worked on it, shifting from your critical, left-brain mode of thought to a more relaxed concentration, allowing your unconscious to help you, to pull up knowledge and experience you had overlooked. You really are that good!

You are and can continue to be as good as the best picture you have ever done. All you need is practice, so you can have consistently fine results.

In a workshop in the 1970s I was hoping to learn some experimental techniques, but I didn't know where to begin. I was surrounded by apparently insane artists, who were crumbling dirt, sand, and leaves onto enormous watercolor boards and pouring, spattering, and throwing paint and glue every which way. I cowered in the corner, totally intimidated. The instructor said, "Do what you feel comfortable with." This was the result. Now I crave change, but then it was important for me to understand that I wasn't yet ready for a major metamorphosis. *Summer Glow* by Nita Leland. Watercolor, 22" x 30". Collection of Dr. and Mrs. Thomas J. Thomas.

Critiquing Your Work

Sooner or later you will evaluate your work. Self-critique is instructive if you approach it right. There are many good things in every painting, so begin by looking for them. Each time you evaluate your work, make a list of questions:

- What is the best thing in this picture?
- Is the value key working?
- Is the color expressive?
- Can I simplify the shapes?
- Is there enough tension/energy in the picture?

Add to this list each time you critique one of your pictures. *Establish criteria that fulfill your artistic purpose and suit your mode of working.* As your objectives change, modify the criteria. Keep the list going as an indicator of growth and development in your work.

But remember to turn the critic off when the creative juices are flowing. You are "on a roll." Don't stop every few minutes to critique. When you find yourself slowing down, that's the time to step back and look at the "big picture."

Give the work time to grow on you. You may be judging it too soon! Examine the piece from a different perspective. Walk away from it for a while and come back with a fresh eye.

Appreciate your own best efforts. Don't compare yourself with others. This is hard to do, especially in a class situation where people with widely differing backgrounds and skills are thrown together. Most people aren't able to do their best work under those circumstances. Tune the distractions out by concentrating on your own work and ignoring what others are doing.

Avoid negative influences. Learn not to be intimidated by the criticism of others. Consider the source first:

- Does this person know anything about art that can help you?
- Is this person sensitive to what you are trying to do?
- Is the criticism motivated by a desire to be helpful or is your critic trying to cut you down to size to eliminate the competition?

When you need a second opinion, find someone whose judgment you value, who will give you an honest critique.

Trust your instincts. Your unconscious makes valid contributions to your art. Allow "accidents" to stimulate creativity. Author Henry Miller was a prolific painter in his spare time. He said:

There is something else to be said about this immediate, spontaneous way of working, and that is this: in such moments, one is playing at the game of creation.

Resist the impulse to "correct" an inadvertent change or small mistake. An "incorrect" line, shape, or color may energize the picture. Make this work for you or ignore it. Attempts to correct a minor flaw may only call attention to it.

Use your source material creatively. Be an artist, not a reporter. Make it personal and meaningful to you—that's what connects with your viewer.

Learn to handle criticism. Most judges and critics try to be fair, but they're human and they have personal biases. A rejection doesn't necessarily indicate a painting is bad, only that different standards were used for judging.

Taking a creative approach to a traditional subject, Hurd stylizes the landscape into an unusual, yet realistic, image. Informal balance, intricate pattern, repetition, line, value, color: design, design, design! *Still Water* by Bill Hurd. Chalk silkscreen, 20" x 26".

What to Look For

If judging art is so subjective, then how does one conclude what is good art? Tough question. The following are guidelines to help you establish an objective basis for evaluating artwork. Not every artist will agree that this is the best way to judge, but these guidelines will help you to be fair and to be aware of the sense of purpose in an artist's work. A strong painting can withstand serious critique.

Look for *content*:

• What is the concept revealed in the image?
• Has this been expressed dynamically?
• Is this an interesting problem with a unique solution?
• Is there wit and character in the interpretation?
• What is the artist telling you about himself or herself?

Look for *design*:

• How has the artist used design fundamentals to express the idea?
• Are the shapes arranged dynamically on the support?
• Is dominance used effectively?
• Is there a feeling that nothing can be added or subtracted without impairing the unity of the composition?

Look at *technique*:

• How effectively has the artist used his or her skill?
• Is the artist painting with conviction?
• Are techniques well-integrated or just surface tricks?
• Does expertise overshadow meaning?

Examine the content, design, and technique in these two fine paintings. Criteria for critique are the same for realistic and abstract art.

Morning Light by Michael J. Weber. Transparent watercolor, 14" x 20".

Magma One by Marilyn Hughey Phillis. © 1983. Ink, watercolor, and acrylic, 30" x 40". Collection of the Ohio Watercolor Society.

Activity

Following the guidelines above, critique these and two other pictures you find in this book—one you especially like and one you don't. Be as fair and objective as you can. Assume that the artists are sincere in what they are saying in their art, even though you may not agree with it.

You're in the Driver's Seat

Style is the imprint of your personality on your art. The way you look at your subject, how you relate it to your experience, what materials you choose, and your manner of handling them all influence your style.

Hans Hofmann said,

Every art expression is rooted fundamentally in the personality and in the temperament of the artist. . . . When he is of a more lyrical nature his work will have a more lyrical and poetical quality; when he is of a more violent nature his work will express this in a more dramatic sense.

Don't force style or you'll never cultivate one. You may be tempted to fit bits and pieces of style from other artists into your work, but it won't work. You have influences, of course, but your own, distinctive style will assert itself in time. When you become deeply involved with the content of your work and throw yourself vigorously into it, style will take care of itself.

Begin by trying everything. ***Take risks.*** Artist/author Mary Carroll Nelson wrote in *Connecting: The Art of Beth Ames Swartz,*

Every artist who evolves a style does so from illusive elements that inhabit his or her visual storehouse, but the actual breakthrough in the privacy of the studio, when one dares to apply paint in a new manner, is a solitary thrill, dependent upon no one else. It is the individual artist who must act courageously in an effort to grow.

You will never know that thrill unless you dare to try.

You probably already have the beginning of a style. Many artists lament their lack of recognizable style, and yet their work can be easily identified when it hangs with other artists' work. Emphasize the distinctive elements, symbols, or features that appear in your work. You are drawn to things that reflect yourself—certain subjects, specific colors, a way of handling a medium.

An acclaimed artist of the 1980s, Nessim is on the leading edge of a new frontier in art: computer-originated fine art. Nessim moves easily from her traditional mediums— oils, pastels, watercolor, gouache, pen and ink—to the computer and back again. The computer is simply a tool, like a brush or pencil. Her style and images retain their individuality regardless of the medium. *Hand Memory* by Barbara Nessim. Computer ink-jet print, 30" x 24".

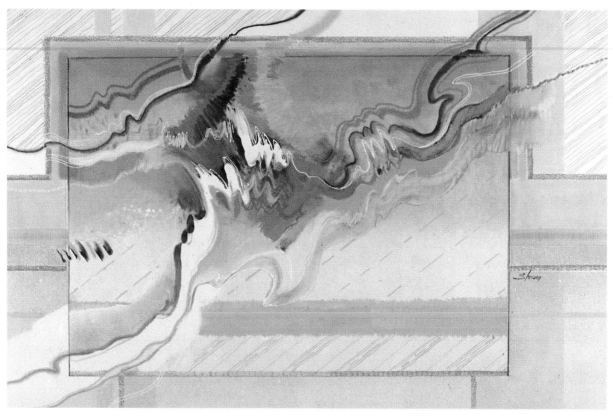

Visualize the process of making this painting, using the steps described here. A "clue" to the concept: Skoczen paints to music. *Breaking Out* by Phil Skoczen. Monoprint acrylic and oil pastel, 24" x 32".

You're Almost There

There are many decisions a creative artist must make. Let's review the major steps involved in making a painting:

1. *Concept*: What do you want to say? You are "making visible" something that cannot be verbalized. Look for symbols that recur in your work.

2. *Composition*: Use the elements and principles of design to support your concept. Look for the best way to say what you want to say. Select the format that supports your idea. Select your color scheme for the creative expression.

3. *Technique*: Master your skills and materials so you can say what you want beautifully. Great technique doesn't make a good painting if you have nothing to say.

4. *Making the painting*: There is more than one "right" idea. Try several plans. Reserve judgment. Don't depend on fancy footwork, but don't be afraid to experiment.

5. *Enjoying yourself*: Value the experience of making art, of learning about yourself and your world. The art is important, but not as important as how you feel about making it. By appreciating the experience, you make the result a thing of value.

The Starting Point

"To begin is the thing, begin anywhere, anyhow," said Henry Miller. Pick up your pencil or brushes and get started! The first stroke is always the hardest, but you'll never get anywhere without it. Robert Henri said, "Those who cannot begin do not finish."

That's the answer, no matter how uninspired you feel. Go to your studio and begin. But there's that awesome white surface and nothing begins by itself, no matter what.

Approach the situation from an oblique angle. Instead of trying to force creativity, structure yourself. Set definite limits: time—ten minutes; size—8" x 10"; quantity— four pictures; theme—sky or flowers, line or color. It's easier to work with bite-size pieces and build up a momentum for larger work while you practice your skills and collect ideas.

When your project is more ambitious, analyze it intellectually. Organize a plan of action: choose medium, design, techniques. Don't look for a single right answer—look for many possibilities. Identify the problem, research it, let it rest for a while, then stop structuring and dive in. Anything goes. Wait till your momentum subsides before you stop to critique. To quote Johann Wolfgang von Goethe:

Whatever you can do, or dream you can, begin it. Boldness has genius, power and magic in it.

Above all else, begin!

Underneath it all is a big sheet of Arches 140-pound paper that was once an intimidating, empty space. Myers began by assembling an assortment of colored papers, some that she tinted and textured herself. Then she arranged and rearranged, glued and stitched (you read that right) her collection to the paper. Myers made it all happen. It isn't magic, although it certainly does look that way. *Fragments* by Carole Myers, N.W.S. Watermedia and collage on paper, 28" x 36".

Other Art Books from North Light

Graphics/Business of Art

Airbrushing the Human Form, by Andy Charlesworth $27.95 (cloth)
Artist's Friendly Legal Guide, by Conner, Karlen, Perwin & Spatt $15.95 (paper)
Artist's Market: Where & How to Sell Your Graphic Art, (Annual Directory) $18.95 (cloth)
Basic Graphic Design & Paste-Up, by Jack Warren $13.95 (paper)
Color Harmony: A Guide to Creative Color Combinations, by Hideaki Chijiiwa $15.95 (paper)
Complete Airbrush & Photoretouching Manual, by Peter Owen & John Sutcliffe $23.95 (cloth)
The Complete Guide to Greeting Card Design & Illustration, by Eva Szela $27.95 (cloth)
Creating Dynamic Roughs, by Alan Swann $27.95 (cloth)
Creative Ad Design & Illustration, by Dick Ward $32.95 (cloth)
Creative Director's Sourcebook, by Nick Souter & Stuart Newman $89.00 (cloth)
Design Rendering Techniques, by Dick Powell $29.95 (cloth)
Dynamic Airbrush, by David Miller & James Effler $29.95 (cloth)
Getting It Printed, by Beach, Shepro & Russon $29.50 (paper)
The Graphic Artist's Guide to Marketing & Self Promotion, by Sally Prince Davis $15.95 (paper)
Handbook of Pricing & Ethical Guidelines, 6th edition, by The Graphic Artist's Guild $19.95 (paper)
How to Design Trademarks & Logos, by Murphy & Rowe $24.95 (cloth)
How to Draw & Sell Comic Strips, by Alan McKenzie $18.95 (cloth)
How to Understand & Use Design & Layout, by Alan Swann $24.95 (cloth)
How to Understand & Use Grids, by Alan Swann $27.95
Living by Your Brush Alone, by Edna Wagner Piersol $16.95 (paper)
Marker Rendering Techniques, by Dick Powell & Patricia Monahan $32.95 (cloth)
Papers for Printing, by Mark Beach & Ken Russon $34.50 (paper)
Presentation Techniques for the Graphic Artist, by Jenny Mulherin $24.95 (cloth)
Ready to Use Layouts for Desktop Design, by Chris Prior $27.95 (cloth)
Sir William Russell Flint, by Ralph Lewis and Keith Gardner $55.00 (cloth)
Studio Secrets for the Graphic Artist, by Jack Buchan $29.95 (cloth)
Type: Design, Color, Character & Use, by Michael Beaumont $24.95 (cloth)

Watercolor

Getting Started in Watercolor, by John Blockley $19.95 (paper)
The New Spirit of Watercolor, by Mike Ward $27.95 (cloth)
Painting Nature's Details in Watercolor, by Cathy Johnson $24.95 (cloth)
Painting Watercolor Portraits That Glow, by Jan Kunz $27.95 (cloth)
Starting with Watercolor, by Rowland Hilder $24.95 (cloth)
Watercolor Painter's Solution Book, by Angela Gair $24.95 (cloth)
Watercolor—The Creative Experience, by Barbara Nechis $16.95 (paper)
Watercolor Tricks & Techniques, by Cathy Johnson $24.95 (cloth)
Watercolor Workbook, by Bud Biggs & Lois Marshall $19.95 (paper)
Watercolor: You Can Do It!, by Tony Couch $26.95 (cloth)

Mixed Media

Catching Light in Your Paintings, by Charles Sovek $18.95 (paper)
Colored Pencil Drawing Techniques, by Iain Hutton-Jamieson $24.95 (cloth)
The Complete Oil Painting Book, by Wendon Blake $29.95 (cloth)
Exploring Color, by Nita Leland $26.95 (cloth)
Keys to Drawing, by Bert Dodson $21.95 (cloth)
The North Light Illustrated Book of Painting Techniques, by Elizabeth Tate $27.95 (cloth)
Oil Painting: A Direct Approach, by Joyce Pike $26.95 (cloth)
Pastel Painting Techniques, by Guy Roddon $24.95 (cloth)
The Pencil, by Paul Calle $16.95 (paper)
People Painting Scrapbook, by J. Everett Draper $26.95 (cloth)

To order directly from the publisher, include $3.00 postage and handling for one book, 50¢ for each additional book. Allow 30 days for delivery.

North Light Books
1507 Dana Avenue, Cincinnati, Ohio 45207
Credit card orders call TOLL-FREE
1-800-289-0963
Prices subject to change without notice.